Becoming Whole Again

Help for Women Survivors of Childhood Sexual Abuse

Becoming Whole Again

Help for Women Survivors of Childhood Sexual Abuse

Dr. Vera Gallagher

Illustrations by
Dr. Jo-Anne Miller

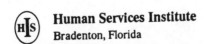
Human Services Institute
Bradenton, Florida

TAB BOOKS
Blue Ridge Summit, PA

FIRST EDITION
FIRST PRINTING

© 1991 by **Vera Gallagher**
Published by HSI and TAB Books.
TAB Books is a division of McGraw-Hill, Inc.

Library of Congress Cataloging-in-Publication Data

Gallagher, Vera.
    Becoming whole again : help for women survivors of childhood
sexual abuse / by Vera Gallagher ; illustrations by Jo-Anne Miller.
      p.   cm.
    Includes index.
    ISBN 0-8306-7657-0
    1. Adult child sexual abuse victims—Mental health. 2. Women-
-Mental health. 3. Adult child sexual abuse victims-
-Rehabilitation. I. Title.
    RC569.5.A28G35 1991
    616.85'83—dc20   91-10639
                                                  CIP

TAB Books offers software for sale. For information and a catalog, please contact
TAB Software Department, Blue Ridge Summit, PA 17294-0850.

Acquisitions Editor: Kimberly Tabor
Development Editor: Lee Marvin Joiner, Ph.D.
Copy Editor: Patricia Hammond
Cover Photograph: Susan Riley, Harrisonburg, VA
Cover Design: Lori E. Schlosser

Questions regarding the content of this book should be addressed to:

Human Services Institute, Inc.
P.O. Box 14610
Bradenton, FL 34280

DEDICATION

This book is dedicated to Rosemary, Sharon, Pat, Gayle, Debi, April, and Terri for reasons they know best, and to the hundreds of women across the United States who have shared with me their lives, their pains, their hopes, and their journeys.

CONTENTS

FOREWORD

Dr. Vera Gallagher has summed up the results of her lifelong work with survivors of childhood sexual abuse. She has called this powerful work *Becoming Whole Again: Help for Women Survivors of Childhood Sexual Abuse*.

I see this book as, first, safe for the therapist and his or her clients. It is helpful for both survivors and therapists in distancing themselves from the problems of childhood pain.

This system of treatment is approached along didactic lines; yet, it is very different from other didactic approaches in that no one is allowed to fail. Should the time and setting not be appropriate, the survivor can choose to wait or be referred to another style of treatment.

This approach studies ideas and concepts. As the memories and the pain emerge, they can be studied and mastered within a supportive group, thus freeing that portion of the individual person's childhood sexuality to unfreeze and develop to that maturity appropriate to adulthood.

Any instrument that can permit study and acceptance with proper safeguards for everyone concerned is by definition a powerful, effective tool. Let me therefore recommend this method to you for study.

Dr. Gallagher has served as principal of Good Shepherd schools in several states. In that capacity, she worked with at least three thousand adolescent girls placed by Juvenile Courts.

The exquisite, forthright simplicity with which Dr. Gallagher writes can only have been acquired through many years of experience.

Joan Davidson, M.D.
Life Fellow in American College of Psychiatry
Seattle, Washington

PREFACE

Last night I met with seven survivors of childhood sexual abuse. All were survivors of incest except one, who had been raped; who, because she had been told to have sex only with the man she would marry, married him. And he made her life a nightmare.

I will always remember Julie. At the first session of our group, Julie walked in bravely, with a short red dress and long back hair flowing free. She sounded good and laughed easily—too easily. What pit of blackness did that rippling laughter shut out? I wondered. Last night she came late—same red dress, only it was dirty. She listened quietly. Would she talk? I wondered. Not without an opening: "Did you have something to say, Julie?"

Julie exploded in tears; tears and a dripping nose for which she had no tissue. Brushing her fist over the tears and under her nose, she cried out, "I was never going to come back. Never. You're all upper middle class. I never knew any of you in the upper middle before. But I gave my word that I'd come back. That's me. Right on the spot, if I said so. I never lived like you. I lived in a dingy, hot little apartment in the worst section of New York. We didn't pretend there; we said things the way they are. I slept in a bed filled with cockroaches and turned on the light at night so the cockroaches would run away into the mattress.

"Here was my bed. And here was my grandmother's and there was my grandfather's. He came over to my bed lots of nights for sex. He'd leave his wallet there with the five and ten dollar bills sticking out. Afterward I'd take one. I was a thief. I took the money. All those years. Now I feel like I want to be a prostitute. Men are attracted to me, and I to them. I could make hundreds in a night and have nice clothes. I feel it. I get all the feelings. I'm scared I'm going to be a prostitute."

Julie is a survivor—a survivor in a half-world without pride or bright lights or self-sufficiency, a survivor laden with guilt. She will never have a parade, and her name will never go on a monument. But Julie is alive, struggling for life in body and spirit, even while experiencing hopelessness and despair. She will never make a grand gesture, and nobody will call her a hero—except God, and me, and maybe the other women in our group last night.

That is what real heroism is—plugging on when there is nothing to plug for, standing human in the face of degradation, one ordinary woman among so much ordinariness. Heroes emerge from new molds today, but we are not ready for them. We remember Joan of Arc at the stake, the Mother of God at the foot of the cross, and the virgins martyred because they would not worship Caesar.

Today's heroism is simple survival, an individual who keeps plodding on with dignity, care, and hope in the face of hopelessness, selfishness, and shame; who keeps trying, who fiercely wipes off the tears with a fist, who has not quit.

Modern heroes are persons like Dana. "Oh, yes, I know what it's supposed to be like," she says. "You meet someone dazzling and then you have sex and it's a slam-bang affair with shivers up and down your spine. Only it's not for me. I'm overweight, and my husband is overweight, and sex is not the greatest thing that ever happened to us. Maybe we have it once a week, and I wouldn't mind if we didn't. Frankly, I'd rather cuddle.

"Anyway, my father taught me sex from childhood on—not all about sex; I knew nothing about that. I knew just the sex he wanted, and I grew up thinking that was how you expressed love. I started periods in the fourth grade and thought I was dying. Later we had a movie in school about menstruation. My mother asked me: *Did you see the movie?* When I said, 'Yes,' she said, 'Good,' and turned away. My mother gave me one more word about sex. 'Don't get pregnant; put an aspirin between your knees and hold it there.' She was through.

"My father said, *You do this only with your father—not with anybody else.* But in high school, when boys were nice to me, we had sex. I didn't know anything else to do. So I got pregnant. I was seventeen. My mother and father would kill me, and I didn't have any place to go. I went and talked to a minister. He said I was sinful and evil and bad. He told me I was going to hell, and he described it for me. I went out and got an abortion. My belly still stings from the scars of that abortion.

"But I met my husband, and he was gentle and respectful—to me! We got married and have a family. We moved away from home and my father who told me too much and my mother who told me nothing at all. I can still feel the degradation, the defeat, and the shame. But I'm raising children, and I'm giving them the life I never had."

That is heroism. Not the heroism of death before dishonor, nor the grand tragedy of eviction from the parental home to life for the sake of a child; no, it is a more gentle heroism—a stretching out from ashes to life, the mouth yet too full with ashes to savor victory. The innocence of the child she once was—long lost, withered, gone; out of that death come innocent children instead.

The cost? Who knows? Who cares? Who grieves? "She let her father do it, didn't she?" That ability to strive from out of a spirit stomped into the mud with a father's boot is the heroism to celebrate today; not the courage of the virgin martyr slain with the sword or flung to the beasts, but the courage not to die because she lost her virginity before she knew she had it.

There is Sally who married the rapist because that is what she had been told to do. Physically and mentally brutalized in her parents' home all her young years, Sally dared not march to a different drummer, to unfurl a banner that her father had not ordered her to hold. "You marry the man you had sex with," he said.

Married, the rapist wanted no more sex: no rape, no fun. But he had taught his young wife the pleasure of sex, the thrill, the desire. Why had the desire gone? she asked, bewildered. He did not bother answering, and she did not guess that he was on the streets and in the ditches searching for a sex he enjoyed only with violence. "Let's have a child," she pleaded, thinking a child would bring them together. Reluctantly, he agreed. Then he physically battered and bruised the child. "If we have a second child," thought the wife who had never asked anybody for help and did not know how to find it now, "then he will love us." They had a second child. He beat that one too.

She left.

Then came a shock. Even if the father had abused the children, the court would not terminate visitation rights. The abuse had not been proved; little children cannot be trusted to tell the truth. "Get the opinion of a psychologist." But the psychologist was a child abuser too, and the report was kind to the father. Another psychologist. The court ordered yet another. It came to light that the first psychologist, the one who was kind to the abusing father, had lost his license in a criminal suit in another state. He simply moved and got another license. Why not? It gave him access to children.

And the mother trembles with her children. While the power of her human spirit shivers under the weight of the long years of lovelessness, that fragile spirit still reaches out gently to others in the group. "Here is my phone number," she says softly. "Call me."

That a woman who has known little more than harshness and the coldness of life can offer friendship to another sufferer is the miracle of a heroism that nobody will ever sing.

Seven Christian women tonight, seven survivors, wearied and bone-pained, seek stubbornly for life with a heroism forever unhonored; forever unknown.

Dr. Vera Gallagher

BEFORE THE BEGINNING

- *You are a survivor.*
- *You are good.*
- *Physical and emotional pain are abnormal.*
- *Because you are God's creation you are entitled to feelings of peace and joy.*

HOW TO USE THIS BOOK

This is a book for survivors of childhood sexual abuse, but it is also a useful resource for therapists conducting individual or group therapy. In either individual or group therapy, it is advisable for both the client and the therapist to have, and use as a guide, a copy of *Becoming Whole Again*. Part Three contains a chapter for therapists who are interested in using *cognitive behavioral group therapy*, the term I use in describing my approach. In the *Appendix* I have provided overview and closing items appropriate to each chapter of the text. The closing items, in particular, are designed to stimulate discussions which develop into therapeutic material. Individual readers, survivors still alone, will also profit from the questions appearing in the *Appendix* that relate to each chapter. I have provided empty space for you to jot down your ideas and reactions to the text, symbolically drawn or written.

In Part Two you will also find two chapters which should be read next, after this one, if you are using the book as part of therapy. The chapter entitled, **Beginning: Territories and Turf**, discusses some issues

important to clients, such as confidentiality, and summarizes the six stages of development in therapy. I have also included a letter written by a client that expresses poignantly the transformation of her feelings from fear to gratitude once she found the courage to open up to others who cared. In **Group: A Family of Friends**, also in Part Two, Pearl, a survivor of childhood sexual abuse, describes the kinds of help a woman can get from joining a group. This chapter also includes information about how your feelings of guilt and shame often spring from misinterpretation of your childhood molestation and how the group helps provide relief from your feelings of isolation and alienation.

Which Are You?

Victim or survivor? Which are you?

Survivor, of course. If you were still a victim you would not have obtained this book or begun the task of sorting through your life's stories. Every day the chilling tales of childhood abuse and victimization that I listen to in therapy astonish me anew. Women have sustaining power, a hidden force that enkindles the flame of hope; hope enough to cling to a life scarcely worth the effort. Your determination and struggle into adulthood entitles you to the title: survivor.

Good or bad? Which are you? ("Bad" includes stupid, dumb, worthless, crazy, ashamed, or guilty.)

God made you. God does not make trash. God made you good. That others inflicted evil does not mean that you are evil; on the contrary, the molestations are evil. No person and no words—not a million of them—can make you "bad." In fact, those of us who witness your struggles marvel at your courage. You've survived. You're a living, breathing person. You've reached out for health and wholeness. You've chosen life. Life is God's gift. You are God's gift. Those sentences combined equal **GOOD**.

Sick or well?

Emotionally wobbly, perhaps, but not sick. The premise of this book is simple: dysfunctional behavior is learned in dysfunctional families or foster homes and atmospheres generated by the perpetrators of childhood sexual abuse. What's learned can be unlearned. Productive and fulfilling behavior can then be taught and acquired. The process is one of education and of reverse conditioning.

You may well be physically sick. Moreover, you may know that but never have gone to a physician. A pain-racked body may have been imposed on you in childhood by sadistic sexual abuse. Should you become free of pain, then your system may feel out of sync, ill at ease. I've met hundreds of women crippled by pain: arthritis, ulcers, migraine headaches, tumors, gynecological problems. They suffer silently because they've *always* suffered silently.

If you're in physical pain, see a doctor. Don't apologize for your symptoms. You do have a right to complain——even though that right was not available in childhood. If necessary, get a second opinion.

Human life was designed for a reasonable degree of happiness. To reach out for joy you need a modicum of wellness. Go for it!

Part One

Childhood Sexual Abuse

Let me give you examples of the kinds of dysfunctional families I have encountered.

The Child As Caregiver

Pearl's mother and father appeared to believe that children existed in the family to take care of their parents. By the time she was thirteen, Pearl had a job after school; all the money she earned she turned over to her mother. No matter how much money she handed over, Pearl could not earn enough to suit her mother, who complained nonstop about her poverty. Pearl's father was an alcoholic whose life centered on booze. Both parents beat her physically and often, right up to the time she left home.

Pearl had serious problems with constipation; in fact, she never used the bathroom in her own house because no bathroom had locks, so her father walked in at any time.

Pearl learned that it was her duty in life to take care of her parents. The personal cost did not matter. Pearl worked her way through college, although her parents could have helped her financially. When she got married, Pearl paid for her parents to go with Pearl and her husband on their honeymoon. Pearl always sent Christmas and birthday presents to her parents and to brothers and sisters long after they were adults. Neither her parents nor her brothers and sisters sent any presents to Pearl, and Pearl did not expect any. It was Pearl's duty to take care of her parents, and to take care of her brothers and sisters for her parents.

Pearl did not have any personal boundaries; she never learned how to say "my space" or "my money" or "my family," for example. She could not say, "This is mine." Physically, she still suffers abdominal pains and disorders.

The Child Who Must Be Very, Very Good

In Sherry's family, the children had to be good: very, very GOOD. No child should ever bother a parent. When Sherry and her twin sister's stepfather beat them after an alcoholic bout, they told their mother. The mother was very angry with the children—perhaps because she was being beaten herself and could not cope. Anyhow, from then on the twin sisters became The Enemy, and their mother treated them as such.

The family ran on a schedule. Children went to school and came right back. They never visited anyone, never had an overnight with a friend or relative, never went to a ball game, never danced at a prom, never went on a trip. They went to school, came home, did their chores, and then they studied. Above all, they did not bother their parents.

When Sherry was in ninth grade a physical education teacher invited her to stay after school for sports. Sherry longed for this small breath of freedom. Her mother did not approve but said that if Sherry chose to stay after school she should not expect that anybody would pick her up. She could walk home: five miles. Sherry walked the five miles in summer and winter; long, hard, cold winters. Sherry got an athletic scholarship to college, but her mother said she could not go to college, so she did not. Sherry left home when she got married.

Sherry had two children, and then went to work outside the home, also, because her husband was temporarily unemployed. Later he also got a good job. Sherry went to work early in the morning, got home around 4:00 PM, cooked dinner, helped the children with their homework, dropped into bed too exhausted to think, and the next day began all over again. It never occurred to Sherry that life is not supposed to be this way.

Eventually Sherry became physically ill. She didn't quit work, of course, but she did slowly discover that her life was out of joint. Her physician sent her to biofeedback because he could find no physical basis for severe pains she suffered; from there the therapist directed her to a group for survivors of childhood physical and sexual abuse. Very slowly, Sherry learned that she really does count; that she really deserves a little bit of free time. Because Sherry lacked boundaries, space for her own needs and person, she has put in several years of learning that she really is a person with rights.

No Boundaries

In Helen's family everybody could do whatever they wanted: her father could abuse her; her mother could yell and scream and throw things; her brother could stay away from home and skip school; Helen could drop out of school; anyone could use drugs or alcohol; stealing was okay and, in fact, admirable. Everyone in the family wore whatever suited their fancy, ate what they wanted when they wanted, and used their home like a shelter.

Helen grew up with no boundaries whatever. She did not know how to act in social circumstances, how to dress, what to expect, or what not to expect. Helen had no ability to protect herself, because she did not know what "protection" means. Helen has been raped several times. Although she is in terror of a repeat rape, Helen is likely to put herself in dangerous circumstances simply because she doesn't know what "dangerous" means. She may walk dark alleys at night alone, or she may go out on the streets at midnight wearing bright pink skin-tight tights, boots, and lots of make-up. Like a child who has suffered from causes beyond her control, Helen repeats actions over and over, trying to make sense out of them. If "it" didn't happen this time, she concludes that she must be in control; if "it" does happen, she got paid for it, so therefore it was not rape. Women who were molested as children may appear to take more risks than usual, and do seem more likely to be raped. In fact, however, they have no intention of risking a repeat rape, and may live in terror of rape. Often from dysfunctional families, such women may never have lived in the normal social life of a functional family. I remember Lucille who told me about repeatedly being molested as a child by a perpetrator who was not a family member. Lucille continued, "I had seven children and every one of them was raped." To model for children the self-confidence and assertiveness needed to ensure the integrity of boundaries is a challenge for an adult who, as a child, did not learn how to protect herself.

Questions For Survivors

What kinds of skills do you need to learn?

In a functional family each person communicates directly with the other family member whom she wants to get the message. Who passed messages in your family?

SEXUAL ABUSE: Who? What? Where? When?

• You were only one of many abused children.
• Most sexual abuse occurs in the home.
• A child who looks for love and security is NOT asking for sex.
• Memories of abuse are often repressed.
• Sexual abuse of children cuts across all racial, religious, social and economic lines?

Sexual abuse occurs when an adult uses a child for sexual purposes. This definition includes the production of child pornography. When the perpetrator is a close family relative or trusted family friend, the abuse is called incest.

According to current statistics, one in four girls is sexually abused by puberty; one in three by age eighteen. According to Harborview Sexual Assault Center, Seattle, one in five boys is sexually abused. That estimate might be low; we suspect that more than one boy in five may be sexually abused, but don't know with certainty. (Boys and men may have more reasons than girls and women not to report.)

Most reported abusers are boys and men. However, the reported numbers of girls and women who abuse are increasing. In my experience I hear of abuse by women with some frequency—and my experience extends over thirty-five years.

The reasons for perpetrators to abuse may be various; however, most abusers were themselves sexually abused as children. I hasten to add that most survivors do NOT become molesters.

A Powerful Addiction

Once the habit of sexual abuse of children is acquired, persons who molest children are not easily amenable to treatment; sexual abuse can become a powerful addiction. That sexual abuse be reported is essential for the protection of other children. The report should be made to Children's Protective Services. Therapists, teachers, counselors, and other responsible adults are legally obliged to report.

In homes where sexual abuse takes place, the perpetrator usually sets up the family environment to his or her advantage. The family is usually isolated; they seldom join community, church, or school celebrations. The family often enforces secrecy: NEVER tell outside the family anything that happens within the family. Where the father, stepfather, or other father figure is the abuser, that male dominant person usually rules the home. Nobody dares disagree with dad. The family also may be puritanical and rigid about sex: NOBODY discusses sex, ever. Besides all that, the environment is generally not nurturing; children do not feel safe and protected. The emotional environment may be even more damaging to the child than the sexual abuse itself.

Children are vulnerable to sexual abuse at any age, but three to five is most often reported as the age when sexual abuse began. The destructive aftereffects may last for years, and are sometimes diagnosed and treated as unrelated problems.

Most sexual abuse takes place in the home. Most perpetrators are close relatives. Perpetrators also can be teachers, clergy, counselors, nurses, doctors, or close family friends.

Letters From Survivors

The above brief description can best be illustrated by quotes from hundreds of letters mailed to me by survivors from throughout the United States.

. . . Life is still so hard, Vera. I plug along trying not to feel too sorry for myself, and trying to control the enormous amount of anger at my mother, father, brother, and sister for their sexual abuse of me.

. . . About fourteen months ago I began to have severe pain which drove me into therapy. Then flash-backs came. I was devastated. My father, the incestful offender, has been dead thirty-three years! I have been able to get wonderful therapy but have a long way to go.

. . . I saw you on the Oprah Winfrey Show and want to thank you for your presence and especially for speaking out and saying to forget forgiveness for now and get the pain out. I have tried so hard to forgive while repressing the pain and anger. But now I have learned that forgiveness and understanding come through facing, and release by expressing, the pain and anger. For the first time in my life I feel peace.

. . . We are a happily married couple who have just finished reading your book, <u>Speaking out: Fighting Back</u>. We have been married for twenty-six years. My beautiful wife, Lila, managed to shove her grandfather out of his role as sexual abuser when she was sixteen. Then her father tried to take over. She ran away from home.

In my family—a most religious one, by the way—my younger sister became "Daddy's little girl." Then my mother turned to me as her "little man." I left that house full of guilt, shame, confusion, and feelings of worthlessness. Both Lila and I rescued ourselves. Both of us learned to forage for ourselves. And both of us turned to God for help—we had nobody else.

God answered my prayers when He gave me the best and most beautiful girl in the world to share my life with. What we saw in each other was the love that we so desperately needed, and the goodness. We do jointly see a psychologist who told us that in all his years of therapy he had never seen a more intimate couple with so much love for each other.

The best treatment for childhood sexual abuse is love. When one has been betrayed as badly as we have been, then the fact that another sees enough goodness to love and commit her life to you enables one to survive, and thrive.

. . . My abuse started between ages eight and ten. The perpetrator was an uncle, one whose position in the family allowed him the freedom to enter our home at will. The abuse only stopped when he passed away. I was approximately fifteen. My parents never knew. They died at a young age.

I repressed the entire episode. When memories started flooding back I was so angry that I could scarcely believe the abuse had been real. But the flashbacks, the body and emotional pain, the rage were very real.

My husband and I talked about it; he became a strong stabilizing factor in all this. Then I talked to our priest. He sent me to you, Vera. And from you I learned that my anger is justified. It's all right to be angry. I may not always remember why, but that's okay.

Now I can look back over my childhood without resentment. I have taken control of my life without the fear of someone coming in and taking over as that person did in my childhood.

The main stabilizing force throughout this ordeal is my faith and strong belief in a loving, caring, and forgiving God. I know, to this day, that without that love and guidance I would not have survived.

Feelings

Because of the sexual abuse, the residual sense of guilt and worthlessness, and the isolation and loneliness, survivors often suffer from low self-esteem. But that inadequate sense of oneself is not valid. Because a survivor has probably spent her life telling herself how worthless she actually is, I invite you to change the message.

Could you spend only five minutes every morning looking in the mirror, straight into your eyes, and saying this to yourself?

I'm a good person.
I never caused the abuse.
I love myself.
Good things will happen to me.
People like me.
Life can be enjoyable.
I can make friends.
When I have a reason for anger it's good to let myself
*   feel and own the anger.*
Emotions are good and can be my friends.

A SURVIVOR'S STORY

- *The child's seducer is powerful.*
- *Manipulated by the adult molester, the child is helpless.*
- *The molester usually has more than one victim.*
- *The child-victim's denial of the pain carries into adulthood.*
- *The efforts of the child-victim to win parental love are endless and continue into adulthood.*

Since the close of 1985 I have listened to, and read, the stories of hundreds of women sexually abused in childhood. The author of the letter below gave me permission to reproduce it in this book.

First, some comments.

The author of the letter sometimes writes from the background of adult survivor; at other times she writes from the confused child's perspective. A few paragraphs are related by a child who could not understand concealed motives and underlying behaviors. The child's memories are evident in the description of satanic rituals; she recalls isolated instances, but with a blurring of detail. The child remembers that her mother wanted her own father in the home because she related sexually primarily to him. But from the story, it's obvious that the mother had been sexually abused by her own father throughout childhood, and that he continued to wield incredible power over her. He may have conditioned the mother to experience sexual pleasure only with him. We don't know, and the child-adult doesn't know.

Abusers lie, lie, and lie some more. This woman's grandfather told her that he was sick of sex with her mother and that he now preferred the

child. Regularly abusers compliment the child by comparisons with the adult sexual partner; for example, fathers tell children that their mothers are sexually and otherwise inadequate, but that the children are sexually competent. Apart from the sexual contact, however, abusers tell children that they are bad for "doing it," that if they speak of "it" they will go to jail, or nobody will like them, ever, or that their mothers will be terribly upset and never love them again. On and on. These ugly suggestions poured into a child's mind distort the thinking process, and render the child incapable of telling anybody about the abuse. Moreover, a family abuser is likely to praise the nonabused children in the home so that the child victim perceives herself as "baddest." Said Jay, "My father, who abused me, would suddenly reach across the table during dinner and slap me so hard and unexpectedly that I saw stars. My father was a devout Episcopalian, but when we came home from church he victimized me. I got so confused. Nothing was predictable, nothing made sense. When I was having sex with him I was wonderful; the rest of the time, anything could happen." The result of the confusion is that the child does not dare complain. She's "too bad" to complain about anything. She ought to be grateful that she's alive.

Believing That Abuse Is Normal

Another serious problem with sexual abuse within the family is that the child comes to believe that the abuse is normal. In one example, a mother lined up her three girls every night to examine their vaginas with a flashlight "looking for worms and things" and scraped, touched, clawed, hurt. One daughter needed shots for asthma; the mother learned to give the shot and then injected it painfully. The daughter-adult had never recognized such behaviors as abusive. (In my experience women who abuse tend to be sadistic.)

ONE STORY: CHILDHOOD SEXUAL ABUSE
by Maria

Dear Dr. Gallagher,

I stayed up last night to read your book, *Speaking Out: Fighting Back.*

Although it brought back sick and painful memories, it gave me hope. I feel like the woman in your book who says, "I made it," or rather "*I'm making it.*"

From the time I was three my mother and father sexually abused me. They photographed and prostituted me until I was four and a half.

It began, apparently, because mother got bored. Apparently she had had an affair with her father over the years. I guess she got tired of marriage and three children and wanted some excitement.

When I was two and a half years old, before it began, life was perfect. My family seemed to love me. I was funny, smart, and they laughed. Then "mommie dearest" stepped in (she likes the name, "mommie dearest"). She used me as "bait" to get her father to come and live with us so she could have her affair without raising suspicions. (Later her father told me that he had had so much sex with her that he was tired of her. That's when I became useful.)

I witnessed those two having sex. I witnessed mother having sex with various other men.

A social worker encouraged me to accept things as they were or my father would have to leave home and so would I. Since my father was the only reason that sex didn't go on at night, I shut up. How I wish I could have been removed from that place forever!

Comment: *Some professionals believe so strongly in the integrity of the family that, today as in the past, children lack the protection they desperately need. Maria's letter continues:*

On several occasions mother tried to kill me. She locked me in a car in the summer heat, placed pillows over my face while I slept (I still cannot sleep with a pillow), and made me swallow poisons. Once she tried to stab me with a butcher knife because her father preferred sex with me and she was insanely jealous. I could describe other examples of her cruelty.

Comment: *I doubt that the mother's actions are exaggerated. I have listened to descriptions of mothers' cruelty and attempts to kill the victim several times. Knives are commonly used to terrify the child. The abuser totally ignores and violates safety needs. Maria's letter continues:*

All my life I wanted a horse of my own. Both my older and younger sisters got horses, and they didn't even ask for them—but not me. I was "too bad;" the child-scapegoat.

Mother tried to prevent me from graduating from high school, but I managed it. For graduation my other siblings got cars for presents; I got a one-way airplane ticket and a suitcase. So happy to escape was I that I didn't notice the cruelty.

My younger sister is the product of my mother's affair with her father, but she named the baby after her husband so that he would be too proud to notice the resemblance to which family. Mother started a lifelong campaign to discredit me, saying I have a "wild imagination." They treated me as an outcast, and I became a loner because it hurt to be near my family.

I turned to animals for love, but when my mother saw that I was becoming attached to one, she killed it.

Comment: *This sequence, also, is not uncommon. Again and again a survivor has recalled, sobbing, how a parent killed the dog or cat that she especially loved. Maria's letter continues:*

I learned to maintain a distance between me and anything I loved. I do want, at this time, to become closer to my husband, but intimacy is not easy.

Mother also seduced and had oral sex with my older brother. I know simply because I walked in on them. Now he suffers from serious back problems. My therapist advised me to write to my brother to see if that would ease his pain. I felt the burden of my mother's abuse had overwhelmed him. But he has "forgotten" all about it. Moreover, he showed my letter to my parents who now will have nothing to do with me.

Comment: *Brothers and sisters frequently deny that any kind of sexual abuse occurred with them or in the family. They say the grown-up child who accuses the parents of childhood sexual abuse is simply crazy or lying. They may deny because they have repressed the memory, or because they can't bear any reminder of it. The aftereffects are likely to manifest themselves as physical, emotional, or addictive behaviors. Maria continues her letter:*

My mother wanted to have me committed as "crazy."

I cannot understand my mother's cruelty. She told my father that I seduced my grandfather and she could not keep me from him. She added (I was four and a half) that I was no longer a virgin. She turned my brothers and sisters emotionally away from me.

I was beaten at least twice a week from the seventh grade through to graduation. If mother would even walk behind me I got chills and the hair on the back of my neck stood up. My siblings think she is weird at times, but would lay themselves at her feet. I realize now that I have no family.

Comment: *The above behavior is "scapegoating": blaming and punishing the one selected child for all that goes wrong in a severely dysfunctional family. Maria's letter continues:*

Mother took my virginity in a satanic ritual, or that's what she called it. She saved my virginal blood. She also had my grandfather heat a serving spoon with a candle and burn the inside of my vagina so I would never enjoy sex.

Comment: *Sounds incredible? About two years ago I came across a situation in which the babysitter, annoyed by the baby's crying, inserted an* *electric curling iron into a baby's rectum, and then turned on the electricity. The medical evidence was conclusive, and the curling iron was found in the babysitter's apartment. In court she pleaded guilty. Maria's letter continues:*

They had given me a drug so that I could see everything but not move.

The next morning I was awakened by sheets of searing pain. I jumped straight up and screamed and screamed. Mother gave me more of the drug so I wouldn't hurt, and kept me out of it for a week— during which time she tried to starve me to death. She also did some sort of thing with a frog on a threshold or something so I wouldn't be able to bear children. So far, I haven't. If you could tell me how to change that, I'd appreciate it.

I could continue with the horrors but that's enough.

Even so, some good has come out of it.

Because I was an outcast, I am not like them. God protected me from her and the memories. He has watched out for me ever since. I guess, after all, there was a reason for me being born.

I married a man I lived with for ten years. It's lovely and romantic. And I'm sure it's made mother mad.

My husband is very sweet, loving, and gentle. Somehow I don't feel I deserve him. But, rationally, I know I do. We consider each other our "rewards" for traumas in life each of us has suffered. The only problem is that he thinks I should just ignore the past and forget it. That's impossible, especially when I see a small child and want to cry for the small child I was while the horrible abuse took place.

Comment: *Forgive and forget is dangerous advice; it merely reinforces repression. Repression is the mother of revictimization. Maria's letter continues:*

I did try, for while, being a $100 an hour call girl.

Comment: *Over ninety percent of prostitutes were sexually abused in childhood, usually by father, stepfather, or father substitute. Maria's letter continues:*

I didn't make much because the business was just starting. One day I saw a trick pull up in a station wagon with kids' toys loaded in the back. That was enough. I quit!

I'm writing to you, I guess, because you know your stuff, you don't judge, and I need a note of encouragement. I keep telling myself I'm fine, forgiven, and innocent, but it still hurts.

Is there a way I can stop remembering and caring? I'm trying out a new motto: "I can't grasp it, so I've gotta let it go." Sometimes it works; sometimes it makes me cry. I still love my family, I love mother and have forgiven her, but she won't respond to me.

Comment: *Victims have tried throughout life to win parental love. As adults, they still seek mother-love. That they will ever get it is unlikely, but hope does indeed spring eternal from the human heart. From a therapist's viewpoint, repeated efforts to solicit mother's love are damaging because each ends in failure. Maria's letter continues:*

When I was very small and listened to mother and her father discuss sex, I knew they were both sick; I became a very responsible person. Often, now, I can't relax or let go. I feel that I should always be "doing" something. I can't sit still for longer than five minutes. I worry about everyone and everything. But it's a security blanket; if I'm responsible others don't have to, and that's how I deal with human shortcomings.

Comment: *Because the child had to "take care" of parental happiness from her earliest days, the adult survivor has experienced years of conditioning to "take care" of everybody and everything within her sphere of experience. This effort is exhausting. Maria's letter continues:*

Except for these memories and questions, life is good. I'm grateful to God that He made me, me, and nobody else. I have a nice home. We plan to buy land in a secluded place and build our final home there.

Comment: *From her letter it would appear that Maria's life may not be as good as described, but the survivor has been taught as a child that she does not deserve anything, and therefore the smallest glimpse of light is enough to make her overflow with gratitude. The letter continues:*

Sister, I'm asking for help, but don't know what help I need. I've told you more than I've told anyone. I'm glad to have a person like you to help with my traumas, troubles, and memories.

Questions For Survivors

Has "forgiveness" become an issue for you? Have you felt that you *had* to forgive your abuser? Have other persons who are important to you "blamed" you for not forgiving?

Each of us tends to deny and minimize feelings about abuse. Have you?

The letter describes physical, emotional, and sexual abuse. In which ways were you abused?

The "need" to love family is natural, even though the family abused. As a child or now, have you sought to love abusing relatives and, to do so, denied the abuse?

Each abused person needs to tell her story many times over. Have you told your whole story?

Are you currently in the process of "remembering"? If so, what incident have you recently uncovered?

BOUNDARIES

- *You, too, have rights.*
- *You deserve time and space of your own.*
- *You are responsible primarily for your own well-being and happiness.*
- *We can't really love others until we have first loved ourselves.*
- *The efforts of the child-victim to win parental love are endless and continue into adulthood.*

Rosie dearly loved her mother who died when the girl was only ten years old. Shortly afterward Rosie's father asked her to sleep with him, and then initiated sex. It seemed wrong to Rosie so she asked her father if these actions were really all right. He said yes, that fathers and daughters do this, but she must not do it with anyone else. Because Rosie still felt ill at ease she suggested to her father that they see her parish priest together and discuss the matter with him. "And then," Rosie recalls, "my father gave me the worst beating of my life. Then I knew it was wrong."

By beatings, Rosie's father kept her submissive to him, but she also had to take care of the house, the cooking, and her four little brothers. On the one hand she assumed much responsibility; on the other she was forced to submit.

Rosie did talk to her priest who asked her to find a responsible woman to talk to, and ask her for help. So one day Rosie ran away. The police picked her up and put her in juvenile hall. She was assigned a woman social worker. With a sense of deep relief, Rosie told her story. But the worker did not believe Rosie. The worker told Rosie that she

was a bad girl and was making up stories only to shield herself. Rosie was devastated.

A family investigation determined that Rosie had told the truth. Her father was given a court date. Rosie was informed that the investigators believed her story. Then her father was allowed to visit her in juvenile hall.

He begged Rosie to lie in court. He said that unless she lied he would go to jail and each of her little brothers would be packed off to a different orphanage and the family would be destroyed. Because Rosie felt responsible for her brothers, she lied in court. "Both the judge and the social worker knew I was lying," she later explained, "and I wanted to die of shame—but I couldn't have my brothers separated." Authorities removed Rosie from her own home.

By this time Rosie had no sense of boundaries. Nothing seemed to have a beginning and an end, nothing seemed directly right or directly wrong. What was the truth? What was a lie? Whom could one trust? On whom could a girl count? When would a friend become a foe, or a foe become a friend? For what was she responsible? Should she take care of her brothers or her father or herself? Or all of them? Or none? How? What was sex all about? With whom does a girl have sex? When?

Marta's father was a therapist and her mother a nurse. She lived in a big beautiful house with servants; money was never a problem. But her parents fought, and her father went into destructive rages that often frightened Marta and her brother. Then an uneasy kind of peace seemed forged, with parents communicating with each other only through Marta. About this time Marta's father began teaching her how to perform oral sex. Her brother, who was as miserable as Marta, got into drugs. After he ran out of his allowance, which was substantial, he prostituted his sister for drug money.

Because Marta was afraid he would commit suicide without drugs, she consented to be used. Eventually not even drugs could kill her brother's demons, and he committed suicide. A divorce followed. Marta went to live with her father. More of the same.

Marta left life with father after he committed suicide. And Marta had no personal boundaries.

Her father had invaded her privacy early on. She could never predict what would happen in the home. A night might be peaceful, or her parents might be screaming at each other. No matter how "good" she was she could control neither. She had sacrificed herself to save her brother, and he killed himself. Then she had given her young life to make her father happy, and he shot himself. She had never known who would come into her bedroom, at what hour, or what he might want. Nothing in her life was clear-cut with straight lines. Disasters happened or they didn't; anything could be expected.

Life Without Boundaries

Persons without boundaries seldom feel secure. Life is a game of chance. Beginnings and endings merge into nothing. Family life can be difficult, and so can social life, marriage, work, raising children.

Because work can be defined with some clarity, I'll look at work and the kinds of issues that arise for persons without boundaries.

Persons without boundaries are likely to overwork: to work hard in the office all day and then take more work home, or allow themselves to be swamped with overwork. They may worry about a supervisor and try to smooth over friction points so that the supervisor will be saved from problems. They may do their own work plus half another person's—which that person asked them to do or said she couldn't complete. They may allow themselves to be passed over for promotions because they have made themselves invaluable in one office—and thus get no extra payment nor recognition. In various ways they may encourage others to use them in the workplace. Although they feel silently resentful, such persons cannot complain.

Women survivors without boundaries were usually expected to play some particular role when growing up, and often continue fulfilling that role in adulthood. They may, for instance, have become the scapegoat, the little mother, the little wife, the juvenile delinquent, the make-everybody-happy child, the good student, the brilliant child on whom the family's honor depends, the liar, the "crazy kid," the sex object, the plaything, the chronic failure, the joker, the picker-upper, the sex addict, the "fatty," the druggy, the dysfunctional child who makes everybody else fail.

J. has written a brilliant description of an adult without boundaries. To J., an artist with words, my thanks.

WHO AM I?
by J.

My favorite and most reliable coping mechanism has been to joke about my pain. Playing the clown was a role I adopted early. In my family it became my job, and my responsibility, to ease everyone else's burdens through my gift of humor. Quickly I developed a sharp wit. I could play on words and seek out the double meanings faster than anyone. I soon became a mistress of understatement. My humor has served me well these many years. Friends plead with me, "Don't ever lose it!" No, I won't; I can't. For if I did, I would be defenseless against the onslaught of deep pain. As many other "survivors" before me have said, "If I wasn't laughing, I'd be crying."

I have no idea of who I really am. I feel as though I am an imposter, because I so often take my cues about how to be in a situation from whomever I'm with. I worry constantly about how others receive me and am very uncomfortable with silence, for it gives me no clues on my performance. This is where my sense of humor is a lifesaver. For I can always tell someone that I am not serious if they are not receptive to my comment or opinion. This illustrates my lack of belief that I'll be taken at face value by another. It is as though I always must be on stage, for if they should happen to be so unfortunate as to glimpse the real me, they'll surely run screaming into the dark night. I sometimes feel as though my presence to another is parasitic. I fancy myself occasionally as an amoeba, slithering along and slimily touching others.

Thus I have very low self-esteem. I allow myself to be used by others, for I think that perhaps they will like me better if I am always there for them. And yet it angers me, for I can perceive that they are using me, but I know not how to escape. I remain totally unable to confront another who is using me or crossing that boundary in some manner. This increases my anger at both myself and the other, and perpetuates my sense of isolation. For every time it occurs, I swear to myself that I'll never let it happen again, and the only way I know of to prevent such a repeat injustice is to avoid the other. Further, it feeds the inconsolable rage that exists inside.

It seems sensible, this idea, that I begin and end somewhere; that is, that I have boundaries. But I fail to see where I end and the other begins. Especially in a close relationship, I want to jump in and "fix" all their problems. I want to be so special to them that they will never leave me. I so fear being alone! But, in all my scheming and controlling, I become disgustingly dependent on the other, and then I feel very hurt when I discover that they resent this behavior (if they are a healthy person. If they are unhealthy, they go blithely along using me until I explode in a rage). I then get angry at them for what I perceive as their failure to appreciate me. Whatever it is called, my acting like an immature child does not engender long-term relationships. Another kind of using occurs when another has shown me any kindness. I am then feeling so grateful and indebted to them, that I pull all stops to repay their perceived gratuity. This causes me to feel somehow obligated for their kindness, whether real or imagined on my part.

I am angry, but slow to recognize it and terrified to express it. I have sleeping problems; I am afraid to go to sleep, and then I cannot stay asleep. I am

exhausted and anxious all the time, but cannot really point to what it is that is bothering me. When asked, I'll reply, "Everything!" Because it is everything. The abuse I suffered between ages three and sixteen did not end there. I went on to marry an abusive alcoholic. Even when, after nine years, I put that behind me, I was still being chased by my "past." I'll sometimes "space out," forgetting what I said or what another person has said to me. I have years missing from my past, and worry deeply about what is still back there, knowing all the while that if I don't remember, it will continue to run, and ruin, my life. But the remembering is not easy either. It is painful; it is ugly and it is brutal sometimes. But it remains far more healthy to continue into the future for me than to be mired in the past. I have seen what the past has done, and change frightens me, but I'm awfully tired of the pain! Even seeping through my humor, the pain is there.

For me, the most basic dysfunction is the lack of trust. Not only do I mistrust the motives and intentions of others, but I also lack the ability to trust in my knowing what is best for me. I see other people's generosity, even a compliment, as coming with strings attached. I carefully assess what they say, wondering what it is that they "really" want. I find this especially with men, but as my abusers were both male and female, I have this reaction to a great degree with both sexes. Thus I expect to be used, and am not surprised when I am. I only wonder how it is that I keep letting people do it. Often, I muse that there must be a sign on my forehead that says, "Use me!" or "I'm easy!" Further, there is the speediness with which I discount even the most deserved affirmation. I realize that my reaction of doubt engenders feelings of discomfort in the affirmer, but the disbelief springs so quickly to my mind, and face, that I scarcely know I'm doing it. It is very difficult for me to swallow my disclaimer and just say "Thank you" to the compliment.

At the same time, I find myself unable to decide what I want from both myself and others. To me, something as mundane as buying a box of cereal is agony. Often, I have gotten so confused and upset over grocery shopping that I have left my cart, run to the car, and sat there crying. This causes me to criticize myself bitterly using the same words and phrases that I learned as a child. We are all familiar with them: "You're no good!" "You stupid bitch!" "Don't you have any brains at all?" And so on. Of course this causes the already fragile self-esteem to plummet further. I am ashamed to discover that as an adult I have continued the verbal abuse from my childhood. I don't need my parents to scream at me any longer, for I am doing it very well myself—still.

This fragile sense of self. If one considers the truth of the theory that we come to know ourselves through those who know us, I can see how my "self" has come to be so seemingly, inexplicably vulnerable and, to some degree, nonexistent. I don't know who, or what, I am. I feel that it is my place to be for others. It is a seemingly noble aspiration. However, I have not learned the healthy meaning of this virtue. What I have learned is that I am "invisible." My wants, needs, desires, and expectations simply do not exist, for I have never had them met. Thus when I am for others, it is with total disregard of my own boundaries or needs. Indeed, I do not even acknowledge that I have needs, wants, or desires. I used to feel pretty good about this. Then I learned that if I expect nothing, I get nothing. Sometimes I am still not sure what it is that I want or need, but I know that I no longer want to be used as a means to another's end.

ADDICTIONS

- *Addictions are used primarily to deaden pain.*
- *The pain must be worked through in therapy, or in other ways, before addictions can lose their power.*
- *Addictions, even the most stubborn of them, can be overcome.*

Survivors commonly suffer from addictions such as alcohol, drugs, or compulsive overeating. The addiction might have been unconsciously adopted to keep a survivor so obsessed that she is not able to uncover repressed memories of childhood sexual abuse. Frequently persons recovering from alcohol begin to remember the childhood sexual abuse, memories that alcohol temporarily drowned.

In any case, addictions are no real blessing for survivors. And they can be very resistant to control. This is especially true when perpetrators use drugs and/or alcohol to seduce the child. Because of addiction in the formative years, the struggle to recover is made even more difficult.

Put very simply: some cells in the brain, that area that may loosely be described as the pleasure center, under certain circumstances release a natural opiate known as endorphins. Other receptor cells are found in the brain, but their purpose is not known. When, however, a substance is used that stimulates the pleasure center in the thalamus, all of the receptor cells seem to jump into action. The intense pleasure is addictive—but increasing doses of the drug of choice must be used as stimulus.

The following commentary on addiction to drugs was written at my request by Gayle. I had met Gayle three times: once I spoke to her group in a city far from Seattle, once she had made a retreat with me in her own city and, sometime after she had written this paper, Gayle flew to Seattle for a visit.

THE LONGING: THE PAIN
by Gayle

The longing. Wanting to be anything but an addict, wanting to be addicted to life instead of a joint. Needing a joint more than the air I breathe. Wanting the satisfaction of never getting high again.

The drug addiction was born in my young life. I was sexually victimized by my four brothers and their friends. In childhood, they gave me drugs for sex. Now all those memories long repressed (or buried in drugs) are exploding into my consciousness. The more intensely I don't want to feel pain from the past, the more drugs I do.

From earliest childhood I smoked pot. Other drugs came after I was old enough—or dumb enough—to buy them. I did downers by age eleven. My stepfather had a prescription for sleeping pills and I helped myself to them until I got caught, age fifteen. Perhaps I could have gotten help then, but I didn't want help.

The help I'm getting now is enabling me to begin to allow others to love me, me to love myself, and to start glimpsing God's love. Maybe I'll be an addict for the rest of my life. Perhaps not. But I do see things differently now.

I had a rough beginning this year of 1987. In fact, I started it as so many years of my short life: got high on New Year's Day. One more high wouldn't matter, I thought. But it did. I can't find safe enough ground to stand on to get rid of the ugly weed.

Uncovering the reasons for my addictions makes my husband's life and mine upset for hours weekly. I have recalled painful, horrible memories every week for one whole year. I had blocked out the horrors of sexual abuse for such a long time.

I feel relentless anger, rage, toward my childhood perpetrators. I even hurt myself to block out the worse hurt of memories and angers. Staying blown out of my socks keeps me going; then I don't have to face the real reason why I can't stay clean. I have turned to professionals for therapy to help me cope with the pain and the hate—and so I don't have to turn to drugs. But I've got a lot to get through.

I just want to get over my mental craving for drugs. My body can live without whatever drives me to get stoned. During the past four years I have withdrawn from cocaine, alcohol, and every kind of speed you can spell. Downers. Smack. The hardest to stay away from is coke. I have drugged for years.

Two or three years after my marriage I discovered that I was sterile. As always, I saw myself as a useless human person. But sometimes I see glimpses of who I really am: not just a stupid broad who doesn't know anything but how to get stoned. After three serious suicide attempts (got "rescued," dammit), I've been thinking that life might be worth a trial. Just the same, I can scarcely touch on the pain it takes to choose to fire up a joint or a line of coke. I crave only the drugs that ran my life for years. I'm twenty-eight years old and still smoke pot on a daily basis—but not in the quantities I used to when my boyfriend and I made hundreds of dollars dealing drugs.

I did bear a child, alleluia! I long to be a good parent, to need nothing more than my little girl's hand—instead of the joint I hoped to die with last year. I said I could quit. I can quit, and I will quit—someday. Drugs are bigger than anything in my life. Drugs are my future. But if I don't give up using I'll hate myself. I need to get into a program to get clean, but—I'm not ready for a program. I'm afraid of people who want me to trust them. I trusted family, and family got me addicted to pot.

Throughout all the years that my boyfriend and I dealt, drugs are all we ever talked about. Drugs were the only thing we had in common. Buyers were the only friends we knew. I want more for my daughter's life than being hooked on anything except life itself.

Guilt almost kills me every time I light up; the center of my pain is addiction. As long as I live I will remember what my brothers did to me.

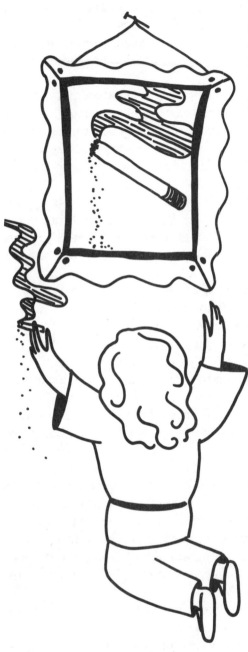

Life is hard, and I need help to get me through. If people would help get me through, I wouldn't need a joint. Maybe you think smoking pot isn't habit-forming. If you think that, pot's choking you to death in its tentacles. Pot does just what drugs do: it makes you an addict. The only thing in my way between being clean and being a junkie is the power of pot.

Just today my husband and I were sitting in our home, knowing that if I could stop getting high we could afford many more possessions. Wanting pot worse is the power of addiction.

Of all drugs, acid had the tightest noose around my neck. My first hit of acid came at age thirteen. For thirteen more years I did at least a hit a week. I have not touched acid for three years, but keep thinking that just one more hit would make me feel fine. And yet, I want a bright future. Bright it will not be without acid.

Courage is not what I need most; I need the *drive* to be clean. Drugs murder the power to choose. I can go for days without pot. I can get over the withdrawal pains but, after several days and months, I always go back. I need the feelings of safety I get from drugs. I need to deaden the angers and pain of childhood sexual abuse. I cannot forget those years. I have to walk through the pain before I can get well. My past is every day of my future.

I remember pieces of me, three years old, getting hurt. I remember bigger pieces of me getting hurt by drugs. Not only was I sexually abused and addicted to drugs, I was socked with verbal and mental abuse too. Even so, I want more out of life than getting stoned.

The longing for children, the miracle of bearing a child has shocked me. I had made myself sterile with drugs; the science of medicine enabled me to have a child. Getting clean might be years away, but I do keep moving, one step at a time.

I can't blame my addictions on abusers any longer. They started it; only I can end it.

Believing in a Higher Power this past year got me further than I dreamed. I had thought that all the bad in me would keep God from forgiving me for all the wrong I've done. Now I realize that God knew my pain long before I did. God gifted me with a child; with the air I breathe; with friends who care enough to help when I need them. But in the end, only another incest victim can understand what I've been through, and know why, and how. In group therapy for survivors, I've found those friends.

I really believe that I can see the end; I can sense the peace. Not the peace of wanting to be dead, but the peace of wanting life. I will, someday, win the war with drugs.

This ends Gayle's story.

Two weeks ago I was in Gayle's city again, and met with her. I had been engaged to give a workshop in her city. Gayle has now been clean for slightly over a year. Gayle is a changed person: happy, laughing, friendly. She is currently working, and will attend college.

Addictions can be overcome—even though the once addict may be always recovering, even though the struggle is hard and long. To Gayle, my compliments and admiration for the courage of her journey.

Are you addicted to alcohol, drugs, food?

How do you struggle with the addiction?

How may years have you had it?

Is your behavior compulsive in other ways?

How are you coping with addictions, if you have them?

STRESS AND PTSD

- *The body remembers.*
- *Survivors experience flashbacks.*
- *Survivors have an overwhelming sense of guilt and shame.*
- *Fears can be overwhelming.*
- *PTSD symptoms mean that you are getting better.*

Within the violence of sexual abuse a child feels helpless, a helplessness often exacerbated by physical violence and threats. The sexual seduction by an adult, frequently a family member, which includes direct physical genital contact or repetitive sexual exposure, is traumatic. Added to the misery is the sexual excitation of a child whose development and immaturity are not prepared for the encounter. The child is thus forced precociously into a world beyond her comprehension; other appropriate developmental needs are ignored.

In my experience such children react in one of two ways.

Two Opposite Reactions

Aggression is a key element in the sexual seduction of children. The child can identify with the aggression and the aggressor, transforming herself from the victim into the rebel. In this case repetition of the deed and the need to reexperience the trauma so as to gain mastery over it gradually come to characterize the victim. Although the youngster is struggling for the upper hand in this situation she may, in fact, leave herself available to other molesters within the family system. Furthermore, the repetition of the incident and the reliving of the super-charged excitement make the child feel guilty, bad, hopeless, and unworthy. The child who stumbles into this method of relieving the trauma of sexual abuse is likely to become a street kid, a juvenile delinquent, a drug or alcohol addict, a permanent rebel against society and its norms.

The opposite choice available to the victim is that of *a massive defense system* that deals with the trauma by denial, minimization, repression, inhibition. This child grows up silent, "good," obedient, uncomplaining, and depressed. She may, as a woman, function well in day-to-day activities, and appear socially adept. But the personal cost is great. Her daily engagements and emotional life are hampered by the effects of the childhood sexual abuse. In the final analysis this person is probably destined to severe neurosis or borderline conditions. She is likely to find sex repulsive and can be described as the typical "frigid woman."

How PTSD Develops

In the first example the child acts out and repeats the trauma. In the second, she represses it. For the time being.

Repression uses up energy. The stress of maintaining it, of living with a sense of guilt and blame, of barricading oneself behind the denial is overwhelming. Eventually the memories force themselves into consciousness, bit by bit, snippet by snippet. The experience can be as terrifying as a thunderous trip on the world's biggest and toughest rollercoaster.

The term used to describe the process that pushes the adult to recover both the memories and the painful reactions that could not be dealt with when they occurred is *post-traumatic stress disorder*

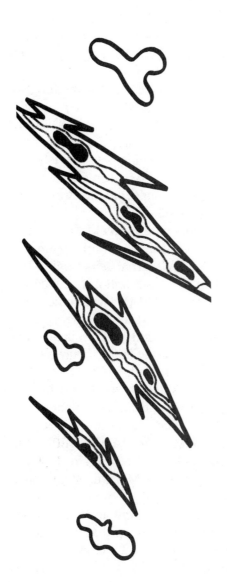

(PTSD). That's the bad news. *The good news is that the adult now has the maturity and ability to cope with the stress.* On the one hand the flashbacks, dreams, nightmares, and feelings that are terrifying cause severe pain; on the other, until trauma has been cognitively and emotionally worked through, it continues to devastate the lives of its victims.

The symptoms of PTSD appear to be organized around reexperiencing, avoidance and numbing, and physiological arousal. There may be physical pains without apparent organic cause, and an exaggerated concern with health.

HAUNTING MEMORIES
by Sharon Gaines

Seven years old, I was taken by my stepfather on his route filling vending machines. Never again would my life be the same. Not by choice, life was changed forever. On that route he initiated the sexual abuse that affected me ever since. For thirty years I kept those memories buried deep within my soul. Totally gone. Forever forgotten, so I thought. Oh, yes, it was there, but buried very deep.

Then one day it happened: a flashback.

Oh God, where did that come from? The memory, the car, the touch, the feeling.

Suddenly I was that little seven-year-old. Not the adult sitting in her living room alone, not the mother with two children of her own. I became the little girl reliving the terror in my life that I could not even believe had ever happened. I wanted to cry out, and yet was silent. Wanted to scream, and was silent. Silence had been pounded into me; I would never say a word.

I am that little girl again, trapped. My voice won't work; I can hardly breathe. I am gripped by fear. I want to move. I am, in that moment, immobilized. I cannot move. Then devastation. Days,

weeks, trying to recover from that memory. Feeling vulnerable again. Feeling alone, abandoned, rejected, dirty. Guilty. Worthless, a worm. "You're no good," I hear. Silently, wordlessly, I cry back, "Your fault! Your fault!"

For years I had suspected that something was seriously wrong with me. But what could it be? Now the fears flood; the horrible sleep patterns, tension, strange and unwelcome feelings, angers, low self-esteem, depression. Something was devastatingly wrong. Now at last I knew the reason for the wrong. Now I knew what had made me the way I was: sexual abuse in childhood.

For the next twenty months my life was chewed up and spit out in flashbacks, body memories, incomprehensible fears, visual hallucinations—I saw what wasn't but had been in childhood. Exhaustion.

As a child I had stuffed the traumatic sexual episodes because I couldn't deal with them, but my body and mind had recorded every touch, sound, and smell coincident with my abuse. They all came back, every single one. Scared.

I hate flashbacks. I hate body memories. The feeling of a hand on my left leg one night when I was in bed, asleep. The leap out of bed. The screams. Heart hammering at my chest. Suffocating, choking. Too frightened to sleep again. Listen to night sounds, turn on lights. Morning, come quick. Daylight, be soon.

I hate muscle spasms in my abdomen. I hate trembling so violently in my sleep that I jerk awake.

Talk to myself: Who am I? How old am I? Where am I? Who am I with? "It's just a memory, Sharon. Get a grip on yourself. Breathe. I'm NOT breathing."

My body reacts to the sound of a power saw grinding away in the neighborhood. Why do I want to run and hide? What's wrong with me? I'm trembling. I'm scared to death. The sound! That's him. The sounds of construction are him. He was always sawing or hammering. He lives in my head. The sound! My body reacts to that sound.

Once, when I did stretching exercises in a yoga class, my legs from the hips down started shaking out of control. I cried, sobbed, howled. Memories. I couldn't describe them, but my body knew. Frozen in fear, I could not move. The instructor came over. "Can you hear my voice?"

Yes, I nod once.

"Can you move?"

No, I shake my head.

"Do you want me to move your legs?"

Yes, I nod.

"I'm going to put my hands on your left leg and move it. Okay?"

Yes, I nod.

"I'm going to put my hands on your right leg and move it for you. Okay?"

Yes, I nod.

"Sharon, it's a memory. I'll sit right here with you until it passes. You're not alone. Do you still hear me?"

Yes, I nod again.

At the end, when I could move myself, I felt exhausted. I could scarcely totter to the car. Home. To bed. Hide under the blankets. The fear registered in every cell of my body is like a saber-toothed tiger tearing body and bone apart.

The burning in my leg and arm muscles never goes away. An unending white hot fire burns in my muscles. Burns from the bone out. Deep within. At nights I cry from the pain. I hate it.

I can't schedule flashbacks. They happen whenever. Wherever. I can be at work, with my children, in church, at a ball game, or driving the car. They come. I'm out of the present, holed up in a space, buried in a nightmare. The nightmare haunts my soul. Sometimes I can figure out what has triggered one. But I don't know how to make the shaking stop. It stops when it's done.

I break out in a cold sweat, nauseated. A recorded memory of fear. Words? I have none. Mental picture? None. Just fear.

Memory. Masturbating him. Me being fingered. A house. A room. A smell. My pubic bone hurts so bad that I double up with pain.

Memories make me sick. I throw up. Fear makes me sick. I throw up. Wake up gasping for air: memory of something in my mouth. Choking. Gagging. Throw up.

I've sat shaking out of control in my home, in my car, in therapy, at work, because of fear.

I don't like my body doing such things. I made the choice to heal. I took control of my life. The memory is one more thing I allow myself to experience because I didn't dare experience it as a child. Some day, some hour I moved from point A to point B, but I don't remember the trip. Don't know how in heck I got here. But I know it's for healing. That's my choice.

Some memories are clear. When he got out of the car I would start shaking and think, please let him lose the car. Don't let him find the car. Please have him be lost. Then I would see him coming back. I would shut down all my feelings and quit shaking and get tense and numb. From then on that's how I lived: tense and numb.

I've discovered that even a drive down certain roads in Indianapolis can revive memories. They were roads I was driven on when a child. I can't get the visual memory, but I remember the roads. My body knows.

I've hurt so much at times that I can scarcely walk. Nothing's worse than reliving those times of terror, and fearing I can't survive.

From my mother: Neglect. Rejection. Blame. I thought she would make the bad daddy go away. Wrong. I had to go numb to stay alive. Don't feel her glare. Don't feel her hitting. Don't feel her tone of voice. Don't feel her hate.

As a child I had no choice. Stuff. Go numb. Feel nothing. Absolutely nothing. Don't feel hurt. Don't feel anger. Don't feel pain. No sadness. Never cry. Never let them know how much they hurt me. Go numb. Leave my body. Look on from outside. Out of the body and not there.

For thirty years numbness has been a way of life for me. I have never been really present until the last two years of my life. Currently I go in and out of numbness. I'm healing at a deep level, but numbness still serves me well at times. But not forever.

I *am* healing. I *will* overcome.

FLASHBACKS: WHAT HELPS

Let the feelings come. The more you fight, the worse they are likely to get.

Try to keep a balance. Keep at hand some work or activity that you enjoy to distract yourself. Remember, you do have control.

Sharon has survived. Others have survived. You can survive, too.

If a flashback occurs when you're driving, pull off to the side of the road.

Use your intelligence to figure out the meaning or stimulus for the flashback. Remember, that childhood situation is gone.

Talk about the flashback in group. Don't allow yourself to stuff feelings.

When feelings are too strong, discharge them: running, swimming, aerobic exercise, punching bag, writing, painting.

POSSIBLE STIMULI FOR FLASHBACKS

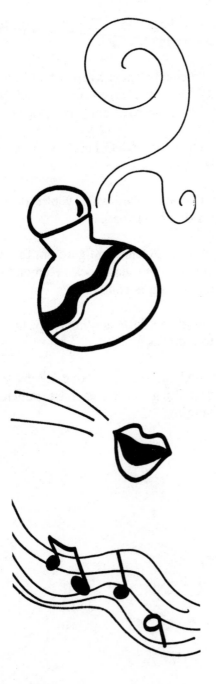

- Perfumes - Smells
- Shaving lotion
- Certain brand of cigarettes
- Color
- Clothing
- Type of body build
- An unexpected touch
- A particular food
- Room decoration
- Area of town
- A victim-like role
- A voice
- A person standing too close
- A touch
- A movie, T.V.
- A book
- Music

WHAT KIND OF PTSD SYMPTOMS DO YOU HAVE?

- Flooding
- Numbing out
- Nightmares
- Stuffing
- Unable to concentrate
- Memory difficulties
- Depression
- Anger, rage
- Intrusive thoughts

PTSD is a delayed reaction to an old stress. The old stress is no longer operative. As an adult you do have control. PTSD is a sign that you're healing; don't allow it to immobilize you. Help is always available:

Call the Crisis Line or Rape Relief.

Learn relaxation exercises: try yoga, TM, or meditation.

Find a group for survivors of childhood sexual abuse.

Visit a mental health clinic.

Seek out a therapist.

LIFETIME EFFECTS of Physical Abuse

- *The origins of free-floating fears are found in childhood.*
- *The reasons for your fears are real: you are not just a silly woman scared of everything.*
- *You need not be victimized by fear for a lifetime.*
- *Resources are available for dealing with fears, and for discovering your own gifts.*
- *Therapy for fears and phobias resulting from childhood brutality can be reasonably short.*
- *The only person who can really heal you is yourself—with a little help.*

I Feel Like a Failure

How many times do survivors of childhood sexual and physical abuse voice these words: "I feel like a failure . . .. I feel bad, worthless . . .. I'm consumed with guilt . . .."?

Physical brutality to children may consume those children, now adults, with fear, paralyzing terror, shame, good-for-nothingness. Hearing the stories of childhood, the therapist can only be appalled at the hidden brutality experienced by thousands of American children every day.

We like to think that every American child goes to a movie once in a while, spends an overnight at the home of a school friend, attends a baseball game, goes to the prom. Not so. Families that sexually abuse children also keep them isolated and often terrified so that reports of the sexual abuse are never made. Such children go to school, come straight home, do chores, study, and go to bed. Year after year after year. When they get older and find a job, all money is handed over to mother.

Again, we like to think that mothers are non-violent, innocent victims of the men they married, unaware of the abuse. Not so. Mothers may be co-conspirators in the abuse, relieved to be rid of their man's attentions. They may be willing accomplices in the physical abuse.

Again and again clients uncovering repressed material remember mothers waving knives and screaming; beating children independent of dad; locking children in dark closets; acquiescing in behavior that amounts to torture. Sometimes mother is the primary punishing parent.

As for dad's brutality to children, it extends beyond the believable: children awakened when five years old with dad holding a pistol to their heads; children tied down and tortured with electric shocks; young girls at puberty chased throughout the house by dad with a belt which he lashes when he gets close enough; children whose bedroom windows are shot out; children strangled so often that they never know which breath will be their last.

Exaggeration? Not so. I've had phone calls and letters from professional persons, including psychiatrists, describing abuse more abhorrent than the above sketch. They called to know if there was a Good Shepherd school in that city in which they could place the child or young adult as she rebuilt a shattered life.

Terror

The overpowering emotion suffered by the adults who were these children is *fear*: a terror that bites at every step lest they make a mistake, fail to attain perfection, even attract any attention to themselves. One client, for example, could not attend the first day of college because she feared her stupidity would show (the young woman is brilliant); another is convinced of her "badness" almost to the point of hopelessness (even though she worked her way through school and is engaged as a nurse in a prominent hospital); another looks at each successful achievement with unbelievable surprise because she had learned that she was "dumb, stupid, an imbecile." *Even though these women can see and touch their achievements, the whole childhood conditioning to failure forces them to disbelieve the evidence of their senses.*

Following is the story of one such person.

I FEEL LIKE A FAILURE
by DeeAnne

During my first years of school my dad was a policeman and he worked late. He came home a few hours before we went to school. My mom got us up in the morning, and while my sister and I were getting ready for school, my mom would give us the details of that day. Then she would leave for work. My sister and I would wake my brothers. My father would be up by that time and he would make sure we were washed and cleaned for school.

Our house had a downstairs. My sister and I slept down there. My mom wanted the boys close to her upstairs because my younger brother was a baby and my mom wanted him close to her. In the morning, my mom would walk to the downstairs door and call my sister and me. We had to sleep really lightly so we could hear my mom's voice when she called. She would only call our names twice, and if we didn't hear her, we would get in trouble. Trouble in our house was big trouble, so I learned to listen for her voice, even in my sleep. Provided that I told myself to sleep lightly before falling asleep, I would hear my mom's voice in the morning.

Once I woke up and needed to race to the bathroom. I was halfway up the stairs when I remembered that I didn't have shoes on. My dad told me that if I didn't have shoes on he would spank me, so I raced back downstairs to get my shoes. But I couldn't hold it, and halfway back up the stairs I had an accident. I started to cry and my dad came.

I had tried to cry quietly, but he heard me anyway, He was really angry and said, "What the hell are you crying for?" I was afraid to tell him. Then he saw the puddle on the steps and snatched me up the stairs and spanked me. I tried to explain what happened but he thought I was lying. Then he beat me all over again for lying and for being too lazy to get up and go to the bathroom.

All of us kids hated to have my dad home in the morning. One of us unfailingly did something wrong. After one of us got hit, the rest knew it was only a matter of time before we got it. He always inspected our uniforms and shoes. Once we were dressed and went into the kitchen it was inspection time. Anyone not properly dressed or with dirty socks or underwear would get a beating.

Once we had passed inspection we could sit down to the table. My dad always made us eat oatmeal. That was Ordeal Number Two. It's not that the oatmeal was bad, but that we had to eat whatever he put in our bowls, and to eat the way he wanted us to eat. We couldn't have sugar because sugar is not good for kids in the morning. Nobody was hungry. I have always been a poor eater so my dad would stand by me. That made me really nervous. I would try to eat, but it stuck in my throat. My dad would order me to eat. I would force myself to swallow but by the third mouthful I could feel that if I ate one more bite I would throw up.

Kids in our house did not throw up at the table. If one did, my dad made her eat it. He made my sister eat it when she got sick at the table, so I knew I couldn't throw up. I would try to eat more and then I would gag. The gagging made my dad really angry. He would go and get his belt. That's when the battle would begin. He'd try to force me to eat, but I couldn't because I was afraid I'd throw up. Then he'd yell at me and swear. Sometimes he'd spank me for not eating, other times he'd just stand there and swear. Every morning this hopeless battle scene was repeated.

I got so nervous that I broke out in shingles, then in hives, all over my body. My dad took me to the doctor. The doctor said that I wasn't eating right and that it was up to my dad to make me eat right.

My dad told the doctor that I wouldn't eat; he had tried everything, but I wouldn't eat. The doctor asked me why I wouldn't eat, and I said because I wasn't hungry. He told my dad to get me to eat and gave him medicine to put on my skin rashes. Then the doctor told me that if I didn't eat I'd get really sick and he'd put me in the hospital.

Every morning for about a month my dad put the medicine on me. He didn't beat me any more at breakfast, but he beat my sister and brother instead.

Sometimes my dad would take us kids to the movies. He would let us invite our friends and we would all go to the drive-in. It was fun, and I wished we could go every day.

My grades were not good in school. My dad sent us to a Catholic school and I was afraid of the nuns. Both my sister and I scored low on our entrance tests so we were placed in the lower classes. I tried very hard to keep quiet and listen in school, but I just couldn't concentrate. I was so tired that it was hard to stay awake.

I hated reading. I was terrified when the class had to read out loud. I'd get so nervous that I'd stumble over every word. I was such a horrible reader that the teacher would allow me to read only one or two sentences. Then she'd send a note home saying that my parents needed to practice with me.

My dad would get furious, pointing out that my brother did fine. Why couldn't I? I really tried, but I couldn't read.

My dad thought my sister and I were dumb and wanted to be stupid. My sister got beat every time she got bad grades or a bad report card. My card wasn't good but it was better than hers, so he would just yell at me. But he interrogated my sister. He must have yelled and beat her for two hours every report card. Then he'd beat each of the rest of us for something else; it really didn't matter what.

Sometimes he got angry because one of us looked at him wrong, or gave him the wrong answer, or because he thought one of us lied or was being smart or had bad table manners. Or anything. Sometimes he would hit a kid during a question-and-answer session just because it took too long to own up to his accusation.

Nobody knew when my dad would be angry. That was the toughest part. Sometimes when my dad was interrogating us my brother would look afraid. When his lips turned white, my dad beat him because he was a coward. Then my older sister would look angry, so my dad would beat her. Then he would turn to me and start a new line of questioning. I got through that fairly well. When my dad asked me what happened yesterday I knew he was fishing for a confession. If he asked me about something I forgot to do, if he asked what I was doing during a specific time period, then he wanted to know about some other member of the family. I learned how to play the game, and often got by without a bad spanking. But it was always touch and go. Never did I last through an interrogation without getting hit, but I usually escaped the bad beating.

Sometimes I'd pass the interrogation fair and square. Then my dad would say he'd still get me later on. When he warned, "You'd better watch out because I'm going to catch you later," I knew I couldn't win. So I gave up and let him catch me.

(My memories are not in order, I'm sorry, so this story won't be in order either.)

While I was learning how to read, my dad tutored me during the summer months. He didn't want to be embarrassed by my poor reading skills, so we'd have tutoring sessions. We'd start after lunch. My dad would tell me the words and I was to read them after him. I started well, but somehow I'd miss a word, and he'd get angry. Every missed word frustrated both of us. Then the threats began. My father said I was just being stubborn, but I wasn't and I really tried. I always missed a word.

Sometimes my dad slapped me every time I said a word wrong. Other times he'd call me names like "stupid idiot" or he'd bang the table and scare me to death.

I'd always end up exhausted and my dad would say, "I'm sick to death of you. If we don't stop I'm really going to hurt you. Get out of my sight." I felt bad. I wanted to learn, but didn't know how.

In school I felt too stupid to learn. No matter what subject, I couldn't get it. I didn't want help from my father, but sometimes he'd ask to see my homework. I didn't want to show it because then we'd go through a question-and-answer session.

"Is your homework done?" he'd ask. "Yes." Then, "Have you double-checked it?" And I'd say "Yes." Then, "Bring it to me." And the battle would begin. He'd check my math first, and I'd pray that I hadn't made a mistake. He would always find a mistake. He'd ask me to look at the problem. Then, "Did you see anything wrong with this answer?" I scarcely knew what to say. If I said yes and the problem was correct, he'd reply, "You didn't check these over." If I said no he'd yell, "This problem is wrong. Why did you lie to me?" I never knew which answer to use so I'd keep still. Then he'd yell, "Answer me!" I'd try something like, "I don't know." We'd continue.

"How much is three times six?" By now I'd be too nervous and frightened to think. "I don't know." But my dad was merely building up steam and I was in for a long session.

The questions kept coming. "How much is three times six?" I'd guess, "Twelve." He'd say, "No! that's wrong. Try again. But this time you'd

better think real hard before you answer. My patience is running out."
I'd think real hard. If I got it right he'd continue correcting my paper; if
wrong, he'd beat me. Either way I lost. The only difference lay in the
number of blows I'd get.

Sometimes I'd get lucky and my sister or brother did something
wrong and my father's attention was diverted to them. If it was bad
enough my father would forget me long enough to jump on somebody
else.

The next day at school I was scared to turn in my homework. I
already knew the teacher would be angry at me. I always felt wrong. I
pretended to understand because I was too scared to say that I didn't. I
felt so stupid. I tried to be perfect in school, afraid they'd see what a
horrible person I was. Whatever they said, I did. Always hovering in my
mind was that dreadful confrontation with my father.

If I were not in trouble, my brother or sister would be. If none of us,
then my mother. When my mom and dad fought we kids went into
another room and listened. If my dad got too angry one of us went to
keep him from hitting my mom. The fights were usually about his
drinking and cheating on mom; sometimes they were about us kids: my
dad thought mom was too easy on us. Actually, I don't remember my
mom's presence and think she was seldom around. She was home but
went to bed after dinner.

On my way home from school in the fourth grade I was hit by a
truck. I was scared my dad would find out. People gathered around and
asked me questions. My sister told them to go away. I said I was okay
so she helped me up. My leg was stuck in a funny position but I hopped
to school. I didn't hurt. I was just scared my dad would be angry.

My sister took me to the office. The woman called my mom. My
mom told her to call my dad. I started to cry. The woman couldn't
understand why I was crying and assured me that my dad wouldn't be
upset. He came to the school and when I saw him I started crying again.
He took me to the doctor. The tendons in my knee were torn but no
bones were broken. I got a cast on one leg and the other was wrapped
with an ace bandage. My dad took me home. He didn't yell at me. He
even carried me into the house. I couldn't believe it. How I enjoyed that
day!

A hurt leg was too wonderful to hurt. My dad let me stay up past
bedtime, watch T.V. with him, and eat popcorn. I loved every second of
the attention. I got more attention on my return to school. Students
wanted to sign my cast. Sister Clair walked behind me when I went

upstairs just in case I fell. The cast was uncomfortable but that didn't matter. I was in heaven.

Everyone said I was lucky not to have been hurt more. I wished I had been really hurt because I would have gotten even more attention, for longer. I wore the cast for two or three months, but the attention didn't last. Everything got the same.

When I was fourteen my parents divorced. Nobody wanted to live with my dad so I did because I felt sorry for him. My two brothers and sister went with my mom. I was terribly depressed, hated myself, was always sick. If I didn't have bronchitis, I had strep throat; if not strep throat, I had the flu. My new stepmother didn't like me. She told me outright that she didn't like me because I was always sick and so negative. I had to babysit my new adopted little sister, with the result that I couldn't try out for track, drama, or any activity because I had to hurry home from school to babysit my little sister and cook dinner. And I was always in trouble.

My dad didn't hit or spank me very much; mostly he just yelled at me. I couldn't do anything right, even though my school grades were okay. I got a few As, a few Bs, and a C, or maybe a D. I just didn't care anymore. I wasn't allowed to see my birth family. If I did sneak off and visit them, my stepmom and my dad would interrogate me. Visiting them was not worth the price I had to pay.

My dad got his B.A. in law and psychology. He was promoted to investigate for the district attorney's office. Then he got a second job with the Equal Employment Opportunity Commission. My dad is smart.

Real smart. He knew exactly how to get to me. For the first few years of his second marriage he acted fairly decent. Then he started getting real nice to me: French-kissing me, coming into the bathroom when I was in the shower (I was not allowed to lock the bathroom door). He always came in before I got out of the shower, then he undressed and waited for me. I hated the routine. As he walked past he tried to rub himself against me. I didn't say anything. I just got more and more angry. He tried to get me into bed but I fought him; if that happened once, I knew, life was ended for me. I'd never escape.

My dad's violence got worse and worse. He'd come home in a rage and throw dishes, food, people—whatever. Then one night I heard him go into my little sister's room. She winced, he mumbled, and he climbed on top of her. My stepmom was at work, and dad was home with a bad back. I couldn't believe the evidence of my senses. Suddenly isolated instances of my life began to flash into focus, and I understood. I was paralyzed, incapable of movement. My dad did this night after night. I felt like I was going to explode.

I reported it, and Children's Protective Services took over. My stepmom and her daughter moved out. My dad was found guilty of rape and indecent liberties. He got two years.

I completed two years of college for an Associate of Arts degree. But it has taken many many years for me even to face what has happened, and much of it is fuzzy with the lines blurred.

I'm often terrified. Terrified of thousands of nameless terrors. Unable to remember several years of my life. Positive I'm a failure.

Will it ever end?

Will It Ever End?

Yes, it does end, but probably not without therapy.

How much therapy? At Shepherd's Associates, Seattle, therapy is time-limited to twenty-one weeks, with another twenty-one weeks available. The therapist is not the healer; *the client heals herself.* With cooperation life can change in a reasonable time framework.

Ask yourself, "Am I always afraid?" and "Of what am I afraid?" *Putting your finger on the original cause of fear enables you to confront that fear and conquer it.*

To concretize the fear-causing childhood incidents by creating figures forever caught in the original assault is one way of dealing with a real fear. For instance, if a child was repeatedly beaten by a father or mother, that child-adult can create a child out of such vegetables as celery sticks, carrot sticks, radishes, cauliflower, red cabbage, bits of lettuce, and then create the adult abuser in the act of beating, using guns or knives, etc. The figure can be quite detailed. Then the child-adult can take the

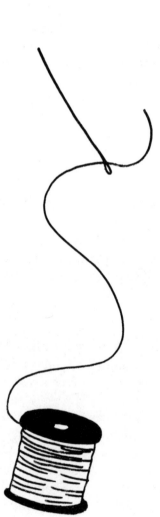

abuser and smash her/him into those fragments that can never be reassembled.

Repetitive actions of this sort can minimize the crippling childhood conditioning to terror, and replace it with some sense of mastery and person-hood. The child-adult can also engage in a variety of opportunities for enrichment to discover hitherto unrecognized talents: embroidery, sewing, furniture makeover (one woman of my acquaintance finds old tables for little cost and turns them into something exotic enough to sell for thousands of dollars; she has become wealthy thereby); folk-dancing; computers; foreign language; writing (most authors "get there" by sticking it out through repeated failures in writing); music; aerobics, etc. Community colleges, parks, recreation centers, and neighborhood groups offer countless possibilities at a low cost. Nobody knows the range of her talents until she tries out every opportunity.

Questions For Survivors

In what can you get involved as a journey of discovery? How soon can you create those stick figures that represent what happened long ago, and will never happen again—unless you allow it?

Have you yet looked though the yellow pages to locate a time-limited therapy? If you haven't, why not start now?

WHY GUILT ?

• *Guilt makes many demands.*
• *Anger turned against ourselves causes depression.*
• *Persons who stuff (repress or ignore) guilt and anger harm themselves.*
• *Therapy groups provide relief for lonesomeness.*
• *The caring power of a therapy group leads a survivor out of depression.*
• *Talking out the pain relieves anger.*

The Beginnings of Guilt

The beginnings of guilt are usually laid in childhood, and may have their origin in nothing that the child has done, but in what the child has perceived. An alcoholic parent, for instance, may be angry, disagreeable, threatening; he or she may "beat up" persons in the household, throw things, complain and yell; the parent may be absent periodically. The child, who does not understand alcohol usage and its ramifications, may conclude that her "bad" behavior is the trigger for the alcoholic scenes, and indeed she may be unjustly accused of having "started it all." Sooner or later the alcoholic parent can be counted on to accuse the child of "stirring up all the trouble in this place." *Because the child certainly does not know how the alcoholic drama began, and feels confused, she is easily made to accept the blame.* Then she strives to be "good enough" so mommy or daddy will never get drunk again; but she can never be good enough to avert the tragedy. Each recurring event drives the overwhelming sense of guilt deeper into the child's psyche. It stays there as a generalized feeling, and the child-grown-to-adult develops with an

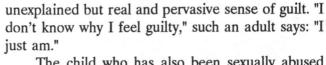

unexplained but real and pervasive sense of guilt. "I don't know why I feel guilty," such an adult says: "I just am."

The child who has also been sexually abused may carry a double load of guilt: "I did bad things and I made daddy (or mommy or whatever adult it was) do it."

Into this fertile seedbed of guilt, today's complex society tosses its arrows; we are not thin enough, deodorized enough, dressed well enough; our skin is not good enough, hair not glossy enough, make-up is a shade off. Or we have the wrong job and run with the wrong crowd and read the wrong books. On and on.

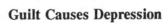

Guilt Causes Depression

With guilt comes depression. Too often depression is anger we turn against ourselves. Actually, we are angry at some other person(s), and rightly so, but as children we were not allowed to express that anger, so we stuffed it, and keep on stuffing through adulthood. One person who got in touch with her guilt, angers, and stuffing expressed herself very well in writing and gave the writing to me. I'm reproducing it here.

Are you in tune with anger, guilt, and stuffing?

"I am an adult survivor of childhood sexual abuse, my perpetrators being my natural father and one uncle—my dad's youngest brother. I was abused sexually by my father from the time I was an infant until I was eighteen years old, got married, and left home. The molestation by my uncle lasted about the same amount of time; the only difference was that it was not as frequent. The last time my dad molested me was exactly one week before my wedding, during which time he cried and begged me not to *leave* him.

"I was a very lonely child. I had no friends. I never trusted anyone because I would never allow anyone to get that close to me. I was a very poor student all through school, very shy, introverted, and kept myself isolated from people as a means of protection. At a very young age I began to steal things. I learned how and when to lie, and I began to smoke when I was only six years old. Most times I would get caught at the stealing—but I just figured that went with the territory. Each time I got caught, I took my punishment and I learned how not to do it better the next time. By the time I was in high school I was quite an accomplished little thief and liar as well. It was a terribly cold, dark, and lonely world I lived in and stealing and lying became the coping skills that I chose to develop as a means of survival.

"I carried the *secret* about the sexual abuse inside me for thirty-seven years of my life until I reached a point in time when I could no longer contain all of the shame, remorse, guilt, anger, grief, resentment, hate, and most of all: that awful feeling of being so terribly alone. I was like this thirty-gallon stock pot full of garbage that somehow got out on the stove with the burner turned up on high. And I know it will inevitably come to a boil.

Knowing that it's going to take quite a while for thirty gallons to reach boiling point, I go on about the business at hand, being a new wife, a homemaker, eventually a mother—what have you—until I sort of forget about the pot I've got on the stove sitting on the back burner on high for a while. Every once in a while I turn off the sweeper, put down the baby, leave the laundry until later, wipe the soap suds off my hands, and go check on the pot—yep, sure enough, it's still there, but it's okay—it's not boiling yet—and then go back to whatever I was doing and get caught up and lost in my lonely little bubble-world again.

"This cycle went on for years—until one day, guess what—the pot boiled over when I wasn't looking and oh! what a mess! This happened in my life in 1985. One night at approximately 7:30 PM I took an overdose and nearly lost my life. I was unconscious for fourteen hours but I didn't die.

"I remember the anger that swelled up inside me when I woke up in that hospital emergency room with all kinds of monitors hooked up to me, needles in my arms, a tube in my nose, and all those faces looking down at me. At first they were all so blurry that I wasn't sure if I were dead or alive. Then I heard familiar voices and felt the tube come sliding out of my nose.

"It was 9:30 AM, and the anger I felt at that moment at still being alive was so great it absolutely overwhelmed me. Immediately I began planning my next attempt—secretly of course. I was so very good at keeping secrets. My dad never raised us to do a job halfway. If the job wasn't done right the first time, we did it over however many times it took until we got it right and it met with his approval one hundred percent. So I knew better than to keep our *secret* halfway. I did it right for thirty-seven years, even after he had been dead for ten years. I was scared to death to tell. In fact, I was much more scared of telling than of dying.

"One point I need to keep clear: regardless of what I did or tried to do, I had no control over that pot on the stove. I didn't know how it got there. I knew I wasn't responsible for it being there—yet I felt that I was. I certainly didn't turn the burner up on high: I was alone, I couldn't scream for help, I could not lift that pot off the stove. The pot was too heavy and I didn't know how to turn the burner off. I felt totally helpless. I knew what was going to happen eventually, but I just didn't know when.

"It wasn't my fault the pot boiled over, yet I was responsible for cleaning up the mess. Nobody could do it for me. I was not to blame for my dad and my uncle sexually molesting me for eighteen years. Yet I felt ashamed, partly responsible, guilty, dirty, ugly, bad, unloved, untouchable, angry, resentful, lonely, empty. Self-esteem was nonexistent and I felt devastatingly helpless. Therefore I absolutely did not care anymore what happened to me. I desperately wanted to die. Everything in my life was dead and lifeless. I was consumed by the aloneness, emptiness, and nothingness.

"I heard about, and later joined, a therapy group for survivors of childhood sexual assault. From that point on I slowly and gradually learned that I am responsible, that I am the one who takes control of my life. I began the process by accepting my feelings for what they are. I learned that if I needed medication to help me get through the healing process, to take it. No more kidding myself that I'm too tough to need help, that I can take care of things alone just because I'd done so for such a long time that doing it alone was the only way I knew. No more kidding myself that I have to be alone in my silent pain because such terribly disgusting and dirty things could never have happened to anyone else on the face of this earth. I am not alone.

"Members of my therapy group cared—but it was hard to trust them. Slowly I learned that they understood exactly what I had had to do to live, and how much I had to suffer to get beyond the *scared* state. Trusting was risky for a long time but, bit by bit, I learned to trust. At that point I was well on my way to healing and wholeness. Beyond the secret. Beyond huge pots on back burners that boiled over when I wasn't looking. Beyond death.

"I began the healing process three years ago. It's taken time to get to the space I'm in today. It hasn't been easy. And it hasn't been fun. But life is beginning to take shape, to mean something.

"Through every moment of this past three years my husband has been very understanding, supportive, patient, tolerant, gentle, and loving. Our four children are stronger individuals because of the pain and suffering they've watched me go through. Today I have close relationships with people I have come to trust and love—true friends—and I can't imagine my life now without these friends who care and love me just for myself.

"As a child all I ever wanted was to be loved for me, accepted by my parents. I wanted only love from my dad, but he couldn't give that. Somehow it all got twisted around, and I'm an adult today who never had a childhood, who was an adult all her life.

"I've cried oceans for that poor little child inside me who never even got to be. But she is alive inside me now and I nurture and love her the way she always wanted and longed to be loved. I've learned from my own children just what it's like to be a child, footloose and fancy free, no cares or worries, no deep dark secrets to keep concealed inside to eat away at her guts like a cancer. My own inner child learns from my children every day. For every inch of the garbage I have waded through and twice almost drowned in over the past three years I can honestly say: it's all been worth it."

The woman who wrote the above has really found happiness and a good life for her husband, children, and herself. Can you have courage to make the journey too?

Hidden Concepts

Hidden in the above story are several concepts that are developed by persons who are overloaded with guilt and therefore believe that they are bad. First of all, in huge letters:

I'M GUILTY: I'M BAD

Then the unspoken but lived-out conclusions:

- I can't get angry (it's my fault).
- I can't ask for help (I'm not worth it).
- I have to be as nice as I can to everybody (maybe if I keep helping they won't have time to see how bad I am).
- If I'm just good enough everything will go right (everything went wrong because I'm so bad).
- I have to be very good to make up for everything that went wrong when I was little (because I was bad then).

These kinds of rules can go on forever *but they can't be kept; they're unreal from the beginning.* They're destined to be broken. And with each "break" their owner gets another dose of guilt. Please select one or more of these rules that apply to you and your efforts to live the good life. Then write down exactly what ways these one or two rules are affecting you today. For instance, in what ways and times do you not permit yourself to get angry: at home, at work, with relatives, with friends, or others?

POSITIVE EMOTIONAL GROWTH

- *You won't recover immediately.*
- *Progress at the beginning of your own journey may seem to move by fits and starts.*
- *You are called on to be patient with yourself.*
- *For now, you must forget forgiveness.*
- *Peace and joy will eventually be yours to claim.*

All growth requires changes, and sometimes change is difficult to make. How often have we excused an adolescent's behavior by saying, "He's just a growing boy!" Or we may say of a child, "She's growing up too fast," with the connotation that such a process must be difficult for her. When we, as adults, are called upon to make changes in our behavior and thoughts, the process is likely to feel difficult.

As long as we live with the false or bad messages given us as children, however, the entire process of living is a challenge. We are, in fact, caught in a two-way bind: painful, often inadequate living according to false tapes; or living through a process of change. The latter option promises the fullness of life; the former ends in a forever dead-end street.

Have you ever heard of jumping in place? That's how one survivor, Sharon Gaines, described her experience of life. Because her reflections were so graphic I asked Sharon to write them down, and then obtained permission from her to make her thoughts available to you.

JUMPING IN PLACE
by Sharon Gaines

Most people think, if they think of it at all, that jumping in place is a strenuous exercise designed to make legs ache, hearts pound, and perspiration pour. It does that.

If continued too long, physical jumping in place can be disastrous. But what of mental jumping in place? The mind's jumping in place is intolerable, suicidal, and meaningless—like the death struggle. I ought to know. Mentally I jumped in place for thirty years. I jumped long enough and hard enough to be an expert, like getting the black belt in judo. But all I got was pain.

The jumping was not meaningless. Because I'm an adult survivor of incest, I jumped in place to survive.

The result was aching joints, and fists so tightly crunched that, in my twenties, I needed thirty minutes after waking to relax enough to get up. Like a roller-coaster hurtling downward, the pain gathered momentum and intensity until I couldn't stand it.

After failing several alternatives, I went to biofeedback sessions. They helped in daytime, not at night. My jaws ached because I clamped them shut all night. One day the therapist asked whether I had been sexually abused as a child.

Bingo! I ducked my head under the blankets as I had done when a child. But I wasn't in bed, it wasn't dark, and I didn't have a blanket. I stuttered the beginning of a lie. But I was never good at lying. "Yes."

She nodded. "I'll offer a suggestion. *Speak the Secret* is the name of a group for sexually abused persons, and it meets in Indianapolis. Joining it might help you. Here's the phone number."

Numb, I took the slip of paper and slunk out of the room, too ashamed to look up. I had never admitted I was sexually abused. Not since I told my mother and was slam-dunked against her cold wall of uncaring. Of anger. Of I couldn't care less.

I stared at the phone number. But I couldn't phone. I couldn't face that ice-cold rejection again. I kept jumping in place.

My mind said, "Face what's happened. You can't continue pretending. You can't fool even yourself." But I pushed my mind down, shoved it under, shut it up. Jumped in place.

But the pain, the aching joints, the clenched jaws got the better of me. I couldn't stand the pain.

I began thinking maybe I could live differently, maybe I could even crawl a bit. Then like a new baby, I began to crawl. Sometimes no movement forward. Just on all fours, rocking back and forth. Pick up the phone, put it down. Call the number. Find out when the group met and where. Do nothing more. Crawl in place. Look ahead sometimes. Glimpse reality; truth, pain, shame. Never head toward life. Do a slow slow crawl.

The woman who answered the phone described the weekly group meetings, the confidentiality. I wanted to attend, wanted to talk, wanted to crawl. To move it.

Three months later I got to the first meeting. Sat there, motionless, a frog on a lily pad. I listened to the others. I wanted to talk but couldn't, my voice as shaky as cream pie. One of the others present couldn't talk either, so I fit in. At the meetings I heard survivors discuss their vivid dreams and flashbacks of childhood sexual abuse. I couldn't.

Couldn't even remember what had happened. But I got committed to the group. *I felt like I belonged.* I listened to people beyond shame. Beyond fear. Beyond rage. Beyond guilt; the perpetrator was guilty, not the child.

The perpetrator was the criminal. He who took advantage of me. He who I believed loved me. He whom I trusted. He who deceived my innocence. He

who enforced silence on me, the child, knowing I'd be too scared to talk. He who used me.

That adult who took from me the good, the true, the pure, and turned it all into a nightmare: he's the bad guy. Not me.

Things moved too fast in group. How could I believe all that, I who had been bent beneath guilt all my life?

It took time to get behind clenched jaws and crunched fists. I absorbed only a small amount at a time. The more my group members talked, the more they made sense. I almost began liking myself.

No! Spit that out! How could I like me? How could *anybody* like me? How could I trust *them*—any of them?

I never trusted anybody. I was afraid of trust. My instinct was to go back to jumping in place. It took less energy than this effort.

I couldn't go back. In group I found persons who really liked me and were concerned. They struggled to find the path that was best for Sharon. I began to talk. I tried to stand, pulling up, off all fours. I wobbled. Confusion made me dizzy. I stumbled, I was afraid of getting hurt.

"Sharon," the group said, "you *have* to hurt. You have to feel the pain and anger. You need to cry."

I can't cry, and I can't feel. I've had no feeling for so long that not even my fingers can feel surfaces; I have no feelings.

I longed to go back to jumping in place. It felt better. At least, I was used to it.

But I had to be alone for jumping in place. I wasn't alone any more. In group people liked me. I felt safe. They listened.

Group members suggested that I find a therapist, and provided several referrals. I contacted a psychologist, and got into therapy. Step by tottering step I walked, walked in pain; the pain of rejection, of no love. Walked in truth; the truth that hurts.

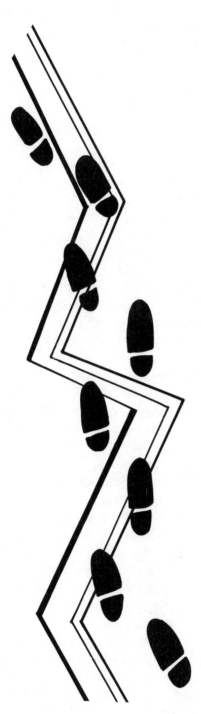

Walked with tears streaming down as I remembered the abuse and humiliations of childhood.

Sometimes shame overwhelms me yet. Then I ask: Would I rather jump in place? No. Jumping in place means all alone. I have friends.

Over a year of group is behind me. I run! I face life, that taskmaster not always fair, not always loving, not always concerned. But I have friends.

I feel joy. I feel sadness. I feel hurt. Sometimes, briefly, I feel healed.

I hated. Can I ever forgive?

Can I cry, I whose tears dried up forever before I was six years old? Can I love? Even love with a deeper and richer love than I might have dreamed?

I have journeyed on a trail of death and life. I have traversed a frontier of the mind, and left dust on the path churned out along the way. The dust will settle. When it clears I'll see the trail, and the person walking on it will be a new me.

I have not reached wholeness, but I've started on the way.

Sharon illustrated very well, I think, the dilemmas that confront the survivor setting out on the path to wholeness. Either you jump up and down, wearing yourself out and getting nowhere, or you jump forward—which means change.

Let me indicate the mental gymnastics of the survivor who jumps in place:

I'll never amount to anything . . .
Nobody really loves me . . .
I'm selfish . . .
I don't do enough for others . . .
I've got to work harder . . .
I'm really just faking it . . .
I'll keep to myself because nobody likes me . .
It's a lousy world . . .
No man can be trusted . . .
I can't be trusted . . .

I made my parents suffer . . .
I've got to do better . . .
I'll try harder . . .
I'm not worth anything . . .
Nobody gives a damn . . .
I'm terribly tired, always tired . . .
I never laugh . . .
I overeat . . .
I drink too much . . .
I might as well be dead . . .
I'm a failure . . .
I have to keep smiling because if I start crying
I'll never stop . . .
I'm bad.

Negative thinking is jumping in place. It occupies our minds but accomplishes nothing. Because, regardless of how hard I try, or what I may accomplish, I still think I'm bad, good for nothing, lazy.

Let me illustrate more clearly.

Are you saying to yourself: "I'm crazy." "No, I'm not crazy." "But only a crazy person could be making these kinds of mistakes at work; could be having these problems with sex; could be anxious; could be so frightened of being attacked." "My therapist said I'm not crazy, but how does she know?" "I'm just pretending to be okay. Well, maybe I can pretend a little longer—if I don't kill myself first."

Can you see that kind of mental jumping up and down, circular thinking, which moves you neither backward nor forward, but wears you out?

Are you able to talk about it? Talking and sharing with the group provides a method of moving forward instead of jumping in place. Eventually you will come to feel that the group members are friends, and that at least you are not jumping up and down in place all by yourself.

You may have a burning question: Why do I feel so guilty all the time? To respond simply: Because

the perpetrator threw the guilt back on you. He—or she—certainly didn't accept any guilt.

Boys and girls who grow up in dysfunctional families seldom are given the love and security they need. Unconsciously, therefore, they walk around looking for love; looking to an abuser, vulnerable. They reach out for love and get betrayal; the perpetrator responds to their need for love by sexual assault. Then the child feels guilty. She was looking for love; she got manipulated sexually. As a result she is likely to think, "It was my fault."

For a child first to invite sexual interplay from an adult is impossible. Sex between consenting adults is appropriate; sex between an adult and a child too young to consent is criminal. Furthermore, sex between an adult and a child is not spur of the moment; the adult planned it, often spent months grooming the child for the encounter, and then took advantage of the vulnerability. Frequently alcohol is involved; that an adult is intoxicated is not an acceptable reason for childhood sexual abuse.

When you read this paragraph, you may not believe me. *If you have felt guilty throughout life, you can't suddenly shrug off guilt.* The process takes time, thought, talking. Writing helps too. I'd suggest that you start a journal, noting memories of abuse as they come.

Memories may not be clear. Perhaps you have no specific memories of sexual abuse, but you have the feelings. Perhaps you have nothing but a suspicion. Perhaps nothing but bad dreams and horrible nightmares. Maybe nothing but overwhelming fears of sexual attack and the need to wear layers of clothing; to wash your hands frequently; to take two or more showers or baths a day; to eat enough to numb out your feelings; to overwork to such an extent that you have no time to think, and so on. If you want to remember but can recall nothing of one or several years of your childhood, then I suggest that you make the best possible use of

group; eventually the memories will come. How long? In my experience, usually within twelve weeks—but not always; depending on the depth of repression, memories may not be immediately accessible.

Usually survivors are afraid to trust anybody because their childlike trust resulted in sexual violation. If you are fearful of trust, that fear is the normal result of a painful childhood experience. And again, you can't learn to trust overnight; please be patient with yourself as you strive to acquire attitudes and emotions that are foreign to who you are.

Sharon Gaines quit jumping in place. She walked. Then she ran. Sharon is now a very well-adjusted woman. She has become an effective public speaker. Sharon is a wife, a mother, and a secretary.

BECOMING A PERSON

- *You are important—as a person.*
- *You need to give yourself time and space.*
- *Watch out for being used.*
- *Love of self is the precondition for love of others.*
- *Develop the talents with which you are gifted.*

Women who grew up in families with one or more persons addicted to the sexual abuse of children have very little sense of themselves as persons. During the early formative years they were used as objects for the pleasure of one person, and often manipulated by the denial of the other. (In most cases the sex addict's spouse tries not to know about the abuse, or denies that it happened, or assumes that the child "made it happen." The spouse thus avoids responsibility.)

The child who is the object of sexual abuse is then taught that she has two parents to take care of: the abuser to whom she gives pleasure (at the cost of extreme pain to herself) and the spouse (whom she protects from unpleasant consequences). The cardinal rule in the house is: *don't tell*. Nothing that goes on in this family is to be talked about outside of the family. The child is forced to maintain the silence and, eventually, to repress even the memories of the abuse.

This child usually matures into a woman who takes care of everybody. From her earliest years she learned that her primary role in life is to take care of whomever she meets regardless of the consequences to herself. Her own pain concerned nobody when she was a child; now her pain does not even concern herself.

Women survivors of childhood sexual abuse get trapped in several different kinds of "taking care of. I've worked with women who took care of the supervisor in the office in which they were engaged; finished up work that others failed to complete; trained new employees; anticipated problems and prepared the office to cope with them. This particular kind of woman never gets a promotion: she is too valuable to the supervisor she's taking care of. Some women take care of their husbands, always selecting a person who is incompetent in some manner so that he needs taking care of. Some allow grown children to live with them, and pay the children's expenses. It's a vicious cycle.

Breaking out of the "taking care of" syndrome can be a difficult and time-consuming process. Because the survivor usually feels bad and worthless, she cannot envision a situation in which her own needs come first.

Eventually the bill of overwork adds up: aching bones, hurting joints, painful headaches and backaches, on and on. The survivor will usually endure the pain until it becomes unbearable. That's the way it was with Sharon.

I AM A PERSON TOO
by Sharon Gaines

In the fall of 1983 I phoned my doctor. I suffered from severe pain in my head, neck, and right shoulder. I thought something was wrong with my ear. The surgeon checked it and said, "Nothing's wrong." I said, "It's gotta be wrong. The pain is killing me." He examined it again. Then he said, "Mrs. Gaines, you need to see an orthodontist about wearing a bite plate. Then contact this person, a biofeedback therapist."

The orthodontist said I definitely needed a bite plate. He said I was tearing my jaw apart from clenching my teeth. If I continued without help I would need surgery on my jaw. I agreed to wear the bite plate. It took the pressure off, so I figured the problem was solved. Wrong.

I tried for three months. My whole body ached when I got up in the morning. My neck burned terribly between my shoulders. My hands and fingers absolutely killed me in the morning when I tried to open them up from a clenched fist. I got up one Monday morning with tears in my eyes as I struggled to open my hands and get out of bed. "That's it," I said. I phoned the biofeedback therapist.

I was so nervous that I could not say my name. I had to hang up and dial again. Before I dialed the second time, I had to get a glass of water because my mouth was so dry that my tongue stuck to it. After several sips of water I again dialed the number. This time I was able to get my name and telephone number out. Then I hung up, sat there, and shook.

The therapist called me back an hour later, and asked how soon I could come in. "How about tonight?" she said. "How about tomorrow night?" I said.

I was nervous about going, but thought I was on my way to solving my problems. It was a casual visit, filling out medical history, etc. I was asked to return next week, same night and time. Little did I know what lay ahead.

The relaxation techniques were fantastic for daytime, but at night my fears took over and I woke up with the same aches. We worked and worked on tapes and techniques. She kept repeating that something very serious had to be wrong.

Would I try to remember? she asked. I sat still, perspiration breaking out on my hands, and I stopped breathing. I had been getting flashbacks about the sexual abuse in childhood. Every time it

surfaced, I shoved it back down. I did not want to deal with it.

For one month I tried to say sexual abuse, but couldn't. It just could not have happened, I told myself. The therapist, I think, knew from the beginning, but wanted me to acknowledge it. She worked with me for ten months. Then she recommended a group, "Speak the Secret."

"It may be just what you need, Sharon, to continue your journey to wholeness. I'm sure a lot is buried.

"Perhaps with other survivors you can allow it to surface." She was right.

Two months into the biofeedback the therapist asked questions about what do I do for me? My husband had been laid off from Chrysler for over two years, but got a job in June. I had had to find work. This is November. My husband and I hadn't done anything together for a long time.

"I can't do things for myself. I feel guilty if I do."

"Do you buy anything for yourself?"

"No, I always buy for the boys. I don't buy for me, ever, unless I absolutely need it."

"Do you buy anything, do anything, for the fun of it? Or give yourself a treat?"

"No, I can't do that. I don't feel like I deserve anything good. I just can't do that."

"You have a new assignment. Do one thing for yourself this week, and for no one else. Pick whatever you want."

I did. Was it hard! I couldn't believe how hard!

Then the therapist said, "Do you have personal time for yourself? Do you take time out after coming home from a full day's work? Take time out for you?"

"There isn't time for me. I do so much for everybody that I have no time at all."

"Why must you do for everybody else?"

"I just do. When I hit the door at night from my job they all start in: "Mom, I need this . . . Mom, I

need that . . . Mom, can I have . . . Mom, can I go . . . Mom, when we gonna eat? Mom, where is my . . .?"

"In other words, you're their slave or maid. Nobody thinks you deserve your own time. I'm not talking a long time frame. Let's say twenty to thirty minutes. No one is to bother you. If he does, a child is to be sent to his room until you're done. If the phone rings, he tells the person to call back later. You can't keep giving to everybody else. Treat yourself well, too."

"I never thought of doing anything good for me. I had to give to everybody else growing up, and I still do."

"As long as you continue, believe me, everyone will take advantage of it.

"You have a new assignment. Announce to your family that you are going to take time for yourself. Tell them you're going into your room and will be there for thirty minutes. You do not want to be asked one question through the door, you do not want to hear your name called through the house, you do not want one interruption for that period.

"Ask if there is something any person must tell you now, because once you close the door, they cannot bother you until you leave the room. Tell them you will set the timer on the stove. When they hear it go off, you will be out of the room. Ask if they understand what you told them.

"No matter what happens, stand your ground. Next week report back to me how it goes."

I thought this should not be difficult to do.

Every night that week I went through all directions and entered my room. I hung a sign on the door: "STAY OUT."

I would set the timer only to hear a child holler, "Mom, I need . . ."

Out I jumped. "What did I just tell you?"

"Oh, I forgot."

"Too bad. Go to your room, I'll set the timer to start over. Until I'm done, stay in your room.

"What if I have to go to the bathroom?"

"You know you're allowed to do that. Then back to your room."

The first week was a nightmare. I got frustrated. I realized they were not listening to me. Needing my time was not important to anyone but my therapist and me.

After only seven days I said to her, "You're nuts. This will never work."

"Did you stand your ground?"

"Yes."

"What happened?"

"Every night this week the boys had to stay in their rooms, and I had to start over every time."

"Did they like staying in their rooms?"

"No, they did not. I don't think it's worth it. But I'm aggravated that they take me for granted, and I can't have even a half hour to myself."

"Next week's assignment is to continue."

"It ain't gonna work."

"Sharon, stand your ground."

"Okay, but I think you're nuts."

Second week and I'm still announcing what I'm going to do, etc.

Third week. One of the boys would holler for me, and then the other would say, "Shut up." Then, "Mom, I didn't mean to say that."

"Sorry," I said. "I accept your apology but go to your room. You have to learn not to call me during this time."

Next week, "How's it going?"

"They know I mean what I say. I hear them discussing it in the living room. If the boys argue among themselves, I hear it. If they call for each other, I hear it. If someone is at the front door, I hear it. Our house is old, not the right floor plan for this adventure. Also, the boy who had done nothing wrong is frustrated at the one who messed up. I started over, and that boy had to wait longer, even if he had not called me."

Again. Therapist: "How did it go this week?"

"You're not going to believe this, but they are paying attention. Each tries to keep the other out of trouble. It's not a total success, but I'm getting somewhere.

"I never realized how much of a difference only twenty or thirty minutes alone can make. When I come out I'm ready to get dinner, help with home-work, answer questions. I listen to a tape of nature, an ocean tape with sea gulls, or whatever, and come out feeling good. Sometimes I take time to read part of a book. I've never been able to read a book. If I tried, I read the same paragraph over and over."

Fourth week. "I've made my point. I'm impor-tant, I have needs, too. I'm not rejecting my boys, I'm just saying that I'm a person with needs.

"When a child wants to play by himself, he does. Whatever goes wrong, he expects me to straighten it out. I explain that it's the same way with me. I am taking care of me."

Fifth week. "When I come home I ask if there's anything the boys need. Says Jarrod, *If we remem-ber later, we will wait until you come out of your room.*

"What happens if you holler for me or anyone?"

"I have to go to my room."

"Jason, how about you?"

"I'm tired of staying in my room. I'm gonna keep my mouth quiet, and I won't holler."

"Okay. Is there anything that you have to tell or ask me? Think real hard."

"No."

I set the timer, put my sign on the door. I had thirty minutes alone.

When I had moved out of the front trenches with my family, I had retreated and won. I had established my rights as a person. I did not ask for much, but I had to fight four weeks for it.

Rules were defined from the beginning. I never strayed from them. God knows I wanted to! I told the biofeedback therapist, "I have gained a major victory. I made myself important. The boys look at me differently now." She was not in the least surprised. She had known that if I just hung in there I could accomplish this for me. I had retreated and won!

It took three more months to gather courage enough to meet with a group. Finally I sought a therapist who could help me deal with the sexual and emotional abuse of childhood.

After an hour's session with my psychologist, Kathleen, I could not go directly home. Instead, I went to Paul Ruster Park. It's a small park by most standards, and out of the way. I wanted to be close to nature, and alone with God. I had many questions for God and myself, and needed time out. I liked the park because it had a long curving driveway that led to an open area. Directly off the park stood a hill. From the hilltop was a view of the valley and a lake, with lots of trees. Alone there I'd cry.

"God, why did it have to happen? God, I'm mad at you. Very mad at you. You can do anything. Why didn't you stop it? I hurt so bad at times. I don't like myself, don't know what I need, don't know what to ask you for. God, what am I gonna do? I'm miserable down here. You know that. What am I gonna do? God, sometimes I want to die. Sometimes I want to run away. God, I'm so confused. Won't you help please. Please. What have I done to deserve so much pain? Why couldn't my mother love me? Why did my mother leave my real daddy? Why didn't she make my bad daddy go away when my sister and I told her what he did? Why did she then hate me and Janet?

"God, I was just born, that's all. I was just born. I never, never asked for this. Why do I have it? I feel close to you only when I'm up here on the hill. I don't know what to do."

Later I realized that God had helped me, but I was too miserable to see it. I looked back over what I had already done. I had gone to the biofeedback therapist. I had asked God to let me know if I was with the right person. I had said, "God, I've got to know that I'm with the right person." And I was.

I never believed I deserved anything. Maybe I do. Maybe I'm even good. Maybe I'll find that out. Maybe I might do something good.

Who knows?

"Right now, God, I need time. I need to be alone. And maybe, just maybe, I need to do some more good things for me!"

Questions For Me

What good things do you do for yourself?

Every day:
Every week:

Do you ever take time to be alone? When? Where?

How many others do you take care of?

Grown children:

Parents:

Adult brothers and sisters:

Nieces and nephews:

Work supervisors:

And:

Do you suffer pain but do not know why?

Where?

Have you seen a doctor about it?

If not, why not?

Do you feel that you do not deserve anything?

If so, who taught you that?

THE FUNERAL OF NOGOOD

• *You are a good person.*
• *The sick child you once believed you were never existed.*
• *The corpse of Neverwas should be buried.*
• *You can forget Nogood forever.*
• *You can devise a ritual to terminate the Phantom Child You Never Were.*

"I'm bad, dirty, guilty, evil, and ashamed."

How many times have you said those or similar words to yourself? How many times have you felt them? All your life?

Chronic child abuse damages the child's concept of self. Because this damage occurs during the formative years, a victim needs to reeducate herself to the knowledge that she is, and always was, a good person.

Because parents or other significant persons used a child for gratification, and because the child hates the sexual abuse, that child has only three options: 1) deny that the abuse ever took place (and repress); 2) change the emotional reaction to the abuse by repeating to herself that the abuse is not painful and in fact is good for her so therefore she likes it; or 3) decide that the abuse occurs because she is bad and if only she would be good such painful episodes would not happen. (When sexual abuse is accompanied by brutal physical abuse the first and third options are usually chosen—unconsciously, of course.)

Physical force and terror are often used to make the child compliant with the perpetrator's desire for sex. Children may be tortured and/or threatened and whipped into compliance. Alternatively, the child may be

controlled by severe emotional abuse. In such cases the victim faces the impossible need to make sense out of it. No longer can she feel invulnerable (as youth generally does) or worthy. In frantic attempts to make sense out of the repeated episodes of terror and her own powerlessness, such a child may decide that she must be bad. If only she were good, this would not happen. But, of course, she can never be good enough. No matter how hard she tries to be good enough, the abuse continues. Eventually, the child assumes that she is irrevocably bad, worthless, guilty, and "nogood." Or she may, on the other hand, decide that the abuse is not really abuse, thus denying the confirmation of her own senses; such a child may learn to dissociate during abuse episodes: "I wasn't in my body; I didn't feel anything because I was outside my body looking on as though it were happening to somebody else."

Families in which sexual abuse takes place in the home and by relatives are dysfunctional. In most cases one parent at least knows that "something is wrong," but does not want to find out what is wrong because then he or she would have to do something about it. So the parent steadfastly looks the other way. A question may be raised also about parents with whom a child does not feel comfortable enough to report sexual abuse by a stranger; in a warm atmosphere wherein parents are approachable, it seems likely that a child would report abuse by a stranger, close family friend, or professional.

In any case, children may be harmed as much by the atmosphere of a dysfunctional family system as they are by the abuse. One woman, for example, reported that every night, when her father came home from work, the children lined up for him to beat each one in turn with his belt. "But at least," she said, "the beatings were consistent; we knew what to expect and when. More difficult were the unexpected and unanticipated beatings by my mother.

. . . My father came into my bedroom every night. My mother had to know what was going on, but she has never given any indication that she knows. In fact, I have heard her deny that any such thing as sexual abuse ever occurred in our home.

To this day I like my father (who is dead) better than my mother. Except for that regular beating, and the sexual abuse, he was kind to me, and he really loved me. My mother never showed any of us the slightest affection. She just had us kids; we raised ourselves.

Often abusing families are rigidly moral and religious. They go to church every Sunday. They contribute, they get involved, they are pillars of the church or community. Or even if they don't go to church they espouse strong moral values: "It's a sin to get angry." "You must honor and obey your parents." "You'll go to hell if you don't forgive." "It's pride to think you're any good and it's pride to develop special talents." Encircled by these impossible rules of conduct, the child hopelessly concludes that she is bad, unworthy, and guilty.

The biggest task confronting the adult survivor is the difficult one of unlearning the repeated lessons of her childhood, of untwisting and unraveling her distorted emotional response, or rejecting the false self-image, of confronting the devastating knowledge that she was used by persons near and dear to her.

The following account illustrates the painfulness of the task, and the imaginative resourcefulness that one survivor used to consign old images to ashes and confirm the new self who is good, capable, and worthy.

TURQUOISE BLANKET
by Sharon Gaines

I jumped awake in flashes of cold cutting light. Star Wars. Tears running down my face. It was real.

The house was on fire with cold flames. I raced to the front door, but couldn't get close. Although I scarcely recognized it, that was my house. No flames attacked outside, but they lashed and writhed within. Suddenly I was screaming at a teenager on the dining room table: "Get out!" An infant lay upstairs. That infant is going to die, I thought, unless somebody gets her. She just lay there. Hearing but not hearing. Lifeless yet alive.

Smoke wrathfully choked the dining room, and the teenager disappeared. The child upstairs died. The fire department arrived. They carried the infant out on a stretcher, a turquoise blanket over her. People stood about in the living room heedless of the devastation.

I stared at the walls. No signs of a fire there. No smoke smell. I kept saying, "This house burned down. What's the matter with you folks? A child died here." Nobody heard. And *where* was the teenager? Firemen had carried out only one body. The baby.

What a powerful dream!

I took each aspect of the dream and lived it. I was the house, the fire, the smoke, the charred infant under a turquoise blanket, I was that lifeless body, yet with life. With ears that hear, yet deaf. With a voice, yet mute. But every time I got to the charred infant on the stretcher I could not, did not, want to revive that child. It wasn't right. That child was destroyed. Burned by fire, cast to the wind, buried in the ground. That infant doesn't belong to me. It belongs to *them*. That child is not me. That child is who I perceived myself to be all those years. The infant on that stretcher is who *they* said I was: dirty, ugly, guilty, ashamed, worthless. That child belongs to *their* minds. *Them*, the ones who abused me sexually, emotionally, physically, mentally. I've lived in that child too long. Give the dead child back to them!

I decided on a symbolic ritual: a funeral. The charred body was part of me, the child who never was allowed to be. The child whose bloated belly was stuffed with lies they taught me about myself: *their* views and attitudes. They lied about me to me. I believed them.

To prepare for the funeral I gathered symbols of the elements: stones of the earth, butterflies of the air, shells of the sea, candles and incense for purification. On black construction paper I wrote out the hurts they had inflicted, the glares, the warped attitudes, the guns, the abuse, the lies. I constructed a small black stretcher of cardboard. I laid the black paper on the stretcher, then covered it with a turquoise baby blanket. The blanket was plain, simple.

The funeral, I figured, ought to take place in my back yard. I would burn the paper and the stretcher. But not the turquoise blanket. (The blanket represented the basic wants of the child, which I never got: gentleness, softness, kindness, love, nurturing, and compassion.) I would let the smoke blow away in the wind. I would bury the ashes in the ground, cover them with dirt, and them stomp on the grave. The end of that distorted portion of my life.

The following celebration would be a pitch-in lunch with food I liked. A gift to me. I would pour life into the vacuum of my soul. Affirmations of my life and accomplishments. Recognition of the distances I have traveled in the healing process. I laid these gifts, typed on white paper, on the turquoise blanket . . . reminders that I can parent myself and celebrate life.

The day of the funeral arrived. It was a pretty day and windy. My friends came. This was new for them, they said, but if I needed it, they were present to support me. I appreciated that.

I had set the table exactly as I wanted. We had lunch first. We enjoyed an afternoon of laughter, sharing, and good old fun. We sat and remembered when first we had come to the group for adult survivors of sexual abuse, and of the miles we had traveled since. Each has accomplished much. We stood in awe of our ability to succeed, even though we never believed we could.

The funeral was scheduled for after lunch.

I took each black sheet of paper and read what was on it, then allowed my friends to suggest memories I might have forgotten. I struck a match and watched the funeral bier burn to ashes. Then I invited my friends to write down and burn their own false selves constructed out of lies. The total experience was awesome, powerful. That black paper did not want to burn, as if it hated to die. But I was determined. Each time the fire went out I struck another match. Then I dug a hole, dumped in the ashes, covered them, and stomped on the grave.

We moved inside to complete the ritual. We took the affirmations out of the turquoise blanket and read them. It moved us to tears—not of sadness, but of joy. *Joy in life that is vibrant, healthy, strong. Life filled*

with love, compassion, feeling, tears, happiness, kindness, gentleness, care for others.

Like the fable of the Velveteen Rabbit, I am becoming real. In the fairy tale the rabbit is noticed for a few brief hours on Christmas day, then is tossed on a shelf and left. The rabbit wasn't held, loved, talked to. The rabbit questions the horse about how to become real. The horse states that one has to be loved, and that becoming real hurts sometimes.

One night a little boy can't find his usual bear to sleep with. The nanny grabs the neglected old rabbit and says, "Here, this ought to do." The rabbit becomes the boy's favorite plaything. It gets worn thin from being held so much. Its ears are dirty from being carried around. Its nose is worn through. It has one eye ready to fall out, but it doesn't mind. Somebody loves it.

Like the rabbit, I had been noticed briefly at the start of my life. But I got holed up inside myself for years and years because of all the abuse. God had placed people in my life at different times to provide a whiff of kindness, enough to keep me struggling on. But I was dying inside: a death nobody could see. Not even me. One night I attended a group for adult survivors of childhood sexual abuse. I walked in broken, ashamed, tattered, worn out from thirty years of attempting to not know the fear, the anger, the rage, the sadness, the confusion, the hurt, the dread of intimacy. Group accomplished for me what the little boy did for the rabbit. The group cared, loved, gave its all for what I needed. Never held back. Carried me along. Accepted me unconditionally.

The journey into reality has been a long, long, winding trail. How many times have I wanted to quit! But a force inside me drove me until I completed the journey. My inner child is now loved by me. She gets the attention, love, and nurturing I once needed. She exasperates me at times. But I love her. Simple, unconditional love. She soaks in it. The turquoise blanket, she loves it.

As of now, I would not trade my life and my journey for any other in the world.

Points For Reflection

What persons constructed your false child-image?

With what words, actions, glares?

Were you as a child physically abused? threatened? manipulated?

Did you come to believe that you really were that "bad" child?

Have you recognized the "Child-Who-Was-A-Lie?"

Are you ready for your false child to disappear?

What symbolic act could you plan to put that pretend-child away forever?

In the future what good things do you wish to do for yourself?

A HIGHER POWER

- *Many persons on their personal journey to healing reach out to a spiritual Higher Power.*
- *The sick child you once believed you were never existed.*
- *Most women sexually abused in childhood have walked away from organized religion because of the hypocrisy of their molester.*
- *Most survivors do, however, retain a deep faith in God and/or a Higher Power.*
- *Some survivors have always known that God walked with them through out the years of pain.*
- *Some survivors begin recovery first with a relationship of trust in themselves, and then with a relationship to a Higher Power—although this search for a Source, a Light, a Peace is always a free personal choice.*

I have never met a person who was self-sufficient, a person not in need of a relationship to some other. Particularly as one begins to heal from destructive lifelong conditioning to pain and silence, she needs another person. At this point many of those survivors turn to God, or a Higher Power. Having survived years of bitter loneliness, persons in group therapy reach out to group members and, often, to a spiritual Higher Power—in whatever way they conceive that Power.

Survivors from throughout the United States have mailed hundreds of letters to me, sharing their experiences. The closer they come to healing, the more likely they are to write about their Higher Power, their Source, or God. For example: "My relationship with the Source is not as

I thought it was. I discovered that I was afraid of God and believed He was out to get me. That's how I felt two and a half years ago. Today I believe in the Light from the Source of all light, love, and goodness in the world. I believe in that Light. I can bring it all around me. I can breathe it in and breathe out the darkness. I have looked into the darkness within, been willing to explore it all, and can fill myself with Light now. I can send Light out to others. Peace is growing inside of me; there is nothing more to fear from within. I feel whole."

Again: "I know God loves me and all others who have been or are going through this same ordeal. God is always in my heart. God has given me the strength to go on in life, not just by myself, but with my family."

From California: "You have no idea of the power of your words on the Oprah Winfrey Show when you said, *Forget forgiveness*. You're a Catholic nun; can you possibly understand the relief I, a Catholic, felt at those words? Through my own bitter experience I've learned that forgiveness and understanding come through facing and expressing pain and anger, not through keeping them all battened down deep inside where they corrode us from within. Fortunately, I found a guide who offered to be a little light on my path for a while. I have walked through the valley of the shadow of death into Light and Love. I have found inner peace and joy."

From a correspondent on the East Coast: "I haven't fully discovered all of God's will. I do know it involves being faithful to my everyday tasks instead of living on the ragged edge. That's a tough assignment for me—yet not hard when done with God. I wish I could tell the whole world about my joy; instead I try to listen to others as they share their stories."

Such excerpts can continue on and on. Suffice it to say that, sooner or later, every correspondent, every client, addresses the God-question. Never do I introduce that subject, preferring to wait for God's touch, that touch that starts off the God-search.

Most of the women around Seattle who ask for group therapy have no religious affiliation and attend no church. Statistically, most women who were sexually abused in childhood have walked away from organized religion, but their concept and knowledge of God in their lives is powerful. Usually they dropped organized religion because their molesters were outwardly "good" church-going people—the church attendance being in reality only a cover to attract trust in their "goodness."

For persons who have been hurt, almost destroyed, by childhood sexual abuse, trust in and intimacy with anybody is impossible. But such persons discover, in the course of healing, that they *can* trust and believe in a higher spiritual Power. After they develop a modicum of trust in themselves, then they turn to a Higher Power to develop a relationship with that Entity as they understand it.

First, they may notice that Higher Power operative in others. They have ventured into group therapy or an all-day workshop, and they observe other women who can be honest, open, and caring. Women in recovery will talk about the danger they were to themselves because of depression, suicidal thoughts, angers—but Somebody or Something called them into relationship with a Source bigger than themselves. Now they are involved in healing; they talk freely, smile at the newcomer, and exchange human dignity with each other.

In the final analysis, each of us is restless until we rest in God, Higher Power, Source, Light—however we understand it. Nobody is truly happy, totally at peace, *because the Higher Power keeps calling us on to higher mountains, more rarified atmospheres*. Especially those who have been hurt, who intimately know their weaknesses, search for Something more. Once a client said, "It sounds crazy but I feel like God loves me more just because I'm such a mess." That theology is right on; throughout Scripture God reveals a predilection for the little ones: those denied justice, the powerless, persons crushed with pain.

Sometimes at the termination of treatment a client will say, "You know, I've still got issues to work on." Every person alive is struggling to become more real, more honest, more truly in relationship with others and with a Higher Power. That relentless journey to total healing—to self-responsibility, self-care, self-nurturing—ends only with death and Life Beyond. So long as we choose Life, we've got issues to work on.

Occasionally faith in a Higher Power is powerful enough to guide a victim of childhood sexual abuse through and out of the bottomless pit. DeeAnne is such a person. She wrote her story.

GOD
by DeeAnne; reproduced with her permission.

I came first to a real knowledge of God, I think, when I was seven years old, and preparing for First Communion. Vividly I recall the words of our teacher: "God loves us!"

How could God love me? I felt unworthy of God's love. At the same time, if only God would love me as, for instance, He had loved St. Bernadette, then I would be okay. I was not, of course, okay now.

Not okay because my brother and a neighbor boy had forced sex on me again and again. I hated it but I dared not tell. God couldn't love a little girl as soiled and dirty as I.

I could tell in confession, of course, and the sin would be washed away. I must tell so that I would be clean enough to receive Jesus in my First Communion. I did try, but the words stuck in my throat and wouldn't get out, and the filth didn't get dissolved away like soiled clothes do.

First Communion day drew ever closer and I got ever more terrified. How could I dress in white, the color of purity, when I was not pure? How could I receive Jesus into a smirched soul? And how could I not go when my father would beat me to death if I didn't?

I prayed and prayed for God to forgive me. All I had to offer was my soul and that I gave up into God's keeping. More than anything I wanted to be used as God's messenger. When my turn came I prayed, "God, if you will use me as a messenger, I will do anything you ask me. I will even give up my family for you." I didn't know what I was saying, and I didn't guess that God would take me at my word. But when I received Communion I knew that I loved God enough to follow His call regardless of where that might lead.

Life at home was bad. My older brother and sister wanted me to play the dog game: strip from the waist down and then my brother would chase us and mate with whomever he caught first. I didn't want to feel like slime anymore so I said, trembling, "I won't play that anymore," and made it stick. My life was not fun after that. My brother and sister tormented me; they sang ditties like, "Isn't she sweet, such a lady fair," on and on. If I went outside they locked the door so I couldn't get back in.

I remember once when I was locked out. I was only eight. It was three o'clock and Mom wouldn't get home until six. I got really upset, thinking I was going to be locked out forever. Frantic, I banged and banged on the door. I talked nice, I got angry and kicked and screamed. My brother and sister just watched me out of the window like I was a freak show. I fell to the ground and sobbed, and they went away for better thrills. Then that mysterious Something—always with me—kicked in and I regained composure. They were not going to make a fool out of me

On the second floor a window was open a crack. I climbed the fence, stood shakily on the top, and jumped to the window grabbing with my fingernails. I stayed right there in my parents' room. My brother and sister got nervous; if I told they would get beatings. They promised never to lock me out again.

But either they picked on me, or my dad did. For trying to be good, I hurt. I stayed alone and played make-believe and kept as quiet as a Russian submarine off the Massachusetts coast. Even so, my brother and sister taunted me, firing their torpedoes into my not-so-silent depths. Where they left off my dad, a policeman, took up.

I lived for school where I learned about God. I loved going to church. God was all that made life liveable. When our family hit rock-bottom, Someone would give me enough energy to carry on. The way my family lived was wrong. In church I heard about love, but there was no love in our house. Our house stunk rotten with yelling, fighting, beatings, sex, hatred, confusion, anger. I had to be the problem, I thought, because nobody else questioned life like I did.

My mom and dad fought as soon as he got in from the night shift; he was a policeman. They started talking low and worked up in volume until they screamed their hatreds at each other. I'd shake with fear. I'd listen in bed. You did not get up in his way if he was mad. We were supposed to be asleep, and we'd better be. You didn't even go to the bathroom if he was mad. You'd keep out of his way because he'd beat up anyone. After he got promoted to district attorney his temper got worse, and he was at home more. That meant he saw more things to beat us up for.

Of necessity we kids drew close trying to bail each other out from under daddy's violence. They were more scared of him than I was so they got beat worse. Many times I'd say I did it—whatever it was—just to end dad's endless interrogations and take the whipping. It didn't hurt, really; I'd pretend I was one of God's disciples. I kept telling myself it didn't matter; nothing mattered. I'd never let them break me.

Dad tried torture too. He'd take away everything I liked. Or he'd make me kneel in the corner, face to the wall, for an hour. If I slumped, or relieved the pressure on my knees, he'd beat me. "You're being punished," he'd yell, "and punishment is supposed to hurt." He made us kids eat cereal with ants in it. They were dead but, when he poured milk on, they floated to the top. I sat there in amazement watching the ants floating around, and mentally preparing myself to eat it. "I said EAT IT!" he yelled. I did. My brother wouldn't, so dad beat him and then spoon-fed him the stuff. No matter, I kept fighting, kept saying, "I won't let him break me." That strength was God.

My dad got a still better job. He was always getting promotions. All this time we had lived in California, and ten years had passed miserably. My sister hated dad, and wanted to move out. He beat her all the time. He was totally obsessed with her. He would follow her when she went out, even to walk the dogs. Once I got between them to stop my dad but he yelled, "Get out. This is between your sister and me." The next hour my head pounded with yells, blows, thuds, screams. I asked God "Why?" I couldn't understand. Why would a God who loves us allow so much bad to happen?

I had been a trooper. I prayed, went to church, clung to life with as much strength as I'd got. I believed in God's promise of eternal life: life without beatings, interrogations, and sorrow. I had thought if only I were good enough life in our family would change, but it didn't. Religion didn't make much sense, but "God," I would say, "I'm hanging in there; you're all I've got. Don't let him break me."

I watched the tremendous hatred of my dad grow in my sister's face. She did manage to escape and explained to me that dad had sexually abused her for years, and she had proof—a package of his love and sex letters! My dad left for Memphis to get himself together and get trained for a new job.

I missed my dad. He was horrible, but I still believed he loved me. It's terrible not to have your dad love you, so I guess I made it up. I suppose I missed the pain, too. You get used to anything, even hurt, until it seems wrong not to hurt. It makes you restless not to hurt. Sounds crazy, but true.

My mom and dad talked about getting a divorce. I didn't want them to get a divorce. What would happen to us kids? Then we moved to a new house when I was twelve, and dad bought some horses. We boarded them at Honey's farm. The farmer's wife was kind and loving; she took me wherever she and her family went. We went swimming, horseback riding, berry picking, even camping. I loved her. I realized that life could be good and that most families were not like mine. She wanted to adopt me, but my parents said no. Honey was a saving grace in my life, a gift from God, a sign that God still loved me.

Dad decided to move to Washington State. Nobody else wanted to. I was in drama, track, a cheerleader, and I was popular in school. Washington State was downhill all the way. My dad filed for divorce. Nobody else wanted to live with him so I went; I felt sorry for him because he would be all alone. Besides that, I'd get away from my brother who kept making sexual attacks.

But my dad wasn't going to be alone at all. He had a future wife already picked out, and she had a three-year-old girl. My dad started trying to molest me: the long kisses, the hard-on when he hugged me, the shower game. I'd go to take my shower but I couldn't lock the door because that was forbidden. My dad would come in and undress and then wait for me to come out. It was totally repulsive. I tried to ignore him, to pretend he wasn't there.

Everything was gone: no more track or drama or cheerleading. I hated school: it was a public school, nobody ever talked about God. I missed my church and Bible study. We lived out in the country, nobody close. I was responsible for cooking dinner, cleaning the house, feeding the horses, and watching my little sister. I felt so alone. Where was God now?

I kept praying. I'm stubborn and I wasn't going to give God up. "God," I'd say, "God . . . you're all I've got." God heard my cry. Into my life he sent a Christian friend, and we got close, even though I couldn't see her except at school; I had too many chores to do.

I graduated. My dad said he wouldn't help me financially with college, but I could live there. Feeling defeated, I hunted for work. I found a forty-hour-a-week job at a big retail chain, and signed up at a community college (thought I was too stupid to get into the university). Then dad charged me rent. I worked full time, went to school full time, fed the animals and took care of my little sister on weekends.

Tired. I drowned in tired. I walked in tired. I studied in tired.

One Saturday I wanted to sleep in. My stepmother woke me up shouting, "You lazy bum! Get up. We're canning today." I couldn't eat enough because she'd say, "You eat all the food." Nothing I did was right. I began to drink.

Whenever he saw me upset or angry my dad gave me a shot glass full of brandy and made me drink it. I learned real well. When I wasn't working for my stepmother, I was helping dad. We worked together fixing fences or cleaning barns and the only thing we had all day was beer. He'd send out for beer for him, and my reward was beer for me. I'd drink with him.

I got depressed. No energy. My grades were poor. All I did was go to school and work and drink.

I never dated. I tried, but by the third or fourth date the guys wanted sex. I'd had enough sex for a lifetime, so I'd say no. Then they dropped me. My stepmother called me a lesbian. I had to be a horrible person, I told myself, for my dad and stepmother to treat me so bad.

Through it all: the drink, the fights, the work, the studies that didn't get done, I became a stronger person. Stronger and stronger. "They will not break me," I said.

My father began molesting my little sister. I got real drunk and then I confronted him. He hit me. We fought and fought. I kicked and pulled hair. He knocked me down and sat on my chest. I wouldn't quit. He pinned my arms and struck me across the face, blow after blow. I didn't care. I was numb. No feeling left. But my stepmother got scared and told him to quit. Then she threatened to call the police. My dad quit and kicked me out.

A year later I went back. My twelve-year-old sister seemed sad, withdrawn, and in a daze. I was worried. I didn't want to move back into that hell but a voice inside me said, "You must help your sister." What's worse, there was another little baby sister too.

"How can I help her? I'm scared. I don't want to." But the voice kept saying, "Help your sister."

I ignored it. I drowned it in booze. But I couldn't stop the voice nagging at me. I moved back.

My dad was sexually abusing my little half-sister like he had molested my big sister, and he was obsessed with her the same way. The voice I didn't want to hear said, *"Get outside help."* But I was scared. I drank all the time now: before school, after school, before work, after work. But the voice kept getting louder. Louder and louder until I thought my head would burst.

I went to a psychologist and told her everything. For days I had lived in terror. She said she'd report to Children's Protective Services. "NO! Give me time to move out. My dad will kill me." But the psychologist said they had to get my little sisters out of there. Frozen with fear, I somehow stumbled home. God, I believed, would protect me. I prayed and prayed for time to move out first.

God came through. He sent a friend into my life. Jerry had me moved out before I knew what happened. When I was ready to drop he would send me a note or come by. My dad was prosecuted; I was the witness, and I did it. He went to jail. Eventually, my twelve-year-old little sister went to a foster home.

At long last my life turned. The foster mother is a recovering alcoholic and a Christian. Her home is perfect. It's exactly what I begged God to give my little sister. She even has horses.

My sister ran away. I was too tired to care. For a whole lifetime I'd tried to take care of my family. It was useless. I gave it up, acknowledging that I couldn't take care of them. Long ago I'd promised God to give up even my family for Him. God had called in the chips.

I zeroed in on my recovery. AA gave me stability and hope. I moved in with that foster family for a year, paid all my bills, got back into a Bible-based fellowship, and initiated my own plans for life.

God has always been and always is there for me. God guided me through desperate fire-storms, and intervened when the need was greatest. When I need strength, God gives strength. God changes dead-end pain into wide-open victory. Not yet thirty, I feel I've lived a long, tortuous life span. What lies ahead, I don't know.

Whatever curves life pitches, God will be there. And God is enough for me.

The material you have read was written at my request. Having noticed DeeAnne's reliance on God, I asked her to write what God means in her life, and she gave her permission to print her story.

Since January 1990 I have seen DeeAnne weekly for individual therapy. She was attending college and feeling so frightened that she didn't know if she could continue. I gave supportive therapy.

DeeAnne was simply terrified. She grew up terrified because of her father's vicious violence and brainwashing. DeeAnne was afraid to ask a question, afraid to answer a question, certain that she is too stupid to learn anything.

DeeAnne was working her way through college, living in a boarding home, and incapable of payment for therapy.

At the close of the school year she won a merit scholarship, all tuition paid for the school year 1990-91. The woman who runs the boarding home has suspended payment for the coming year because she wants to help DeeAnne get through college. For this coming school year the college has offered DeeAnne a part-time job as peer advocate for students. Further, the college is establishing a committee to learn how best the college can help abused women, and has asked DeeAnne to be the primary person on it.

A month ago DeeAnne brought me a check for $1000 to pay for other women who need therapy but are unable to make payment.

Points for Reflection

You have reached the conclusion of the first part of your journey. Perhaps you can pick up crayons or colored pens or pencils and, without planning, let yourself draw symbols for these things:

- the road you have traveled

- the relationship to yourself in trust

- relationships formed with significant others

- your search for a Light, a Source, a Higher Power, God, or whatever you understand a Higher Power to be

- the continuation of your life journey

You don't need to be an artist to sketch in any of the above. I've seen adults paint in stick figures that spoke volumes. If you can't get any ideas, pick up a crayon, hold it loosely, close your eyes, and let your hand go where it will.

You can vary the above suggestions by baking cookies shaped to fit your feelings of the vistas you've seen—or use candy, popcorn balls, pulled taffy, modeling clay, or photographs. The possibilities are endless—as endless as the journey of life.

Part Two

For Survivors *in Group Therapy*

TERRITORIES AND TURF

- *Beginnings call for perseverence.*
- *Groups move through a series of developmental changes.*
- *Therapists are helpers and guides. But only you can change your life.*
- *Total confidentiality is essential for each group member.*

Group therapy is the beginning of hard work and effort. The distortions of a lifetime cannot be remedied within a few weeks. No one of us can make substantive personality changes within a couple of months.

How about confidentiality? Will my confidence be respected? In my experience, confidentiality is the Number One issue for women beginning group therapy. I have led many groups for survivors of childhood sexual abuse, and have never found members revealing the confidences of other women. Knowing the pain such an action would cause, each group member respects the needs of others for total confidentiality. That's important.

Will the group meet my needs? That depends. Many persons molested as children have developed a learned helplessness, or a kind of habitual dependence. A member who joins a group primarily because of helplessness is likely to have only a superficial commitment to group. As long as the leader or a group member is "savior" or "magician," this member is committed. Since, ultimately, nobody can "save" a member except herself, such a person's dependency needs cannot be filled. At that point she may switch to a new "savior," an improved kind of "magician."

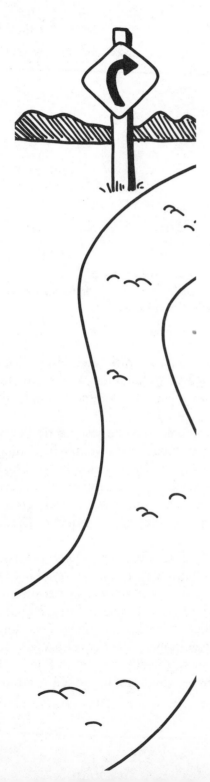

The learned incompetence so often used in the past may now be resurrected for group behavior: "I really don't know what to do. That's why I'm here. *You're* the therapist, and I expect you to tell me what to do. My life and happiness are the responsibility of you, the therapist, or you, the group. You're supposed to change me. If my depression, or my addictions, or my sense of personal worth haven't improved, it's *your fault*, and I'll just have to find somebody or something else." Usually these clients communicate very early that the therapist or treatment is their "last hope," and will the therapist alleviate their symptoms right away, please. Extremely dependent survivors may dramatically exit the present group for a new and more exciting group, treatment, or guru. A succession of such futile expectations may leave her embittered and hopeless, with failures blamed on the treatment mode or the therapist. The real problem is the learned helplessness, the childish dependence. And that problem can be resolved in group provided the survivor is willing to look at and work through the pain of dependency and neediness.

Stages of Group Therapy

Therapeutic groups go through a series of developmental changes that can be briefly summarized.

The *first stage* is that of milling around, feeling confused some of the time, and frustrated. Silences might be awkward, confidence reluctantly and fearfully given.

A reluctance to personal disclosure follows in *stage two*. Members may want to discuss books, movies, or a lecture they may have attended. They tend to introduce various extraneous matter to avoid looking at or talking about themselves.

In the *third stage*, members do begin talking about feelings—but those they have experienced in

the past. They may choose to explore the past at great length, and may indeed need to do so. However, the past can be used as another avoidance technique, eliminating the need for investigation and expression of current feelings about immediate situations and persons.

The expression of negative feelings (*stage four*) shows movement into exploration of significant here-and-now feelings. They can be directed toward the group in general, other members, and/or the therapist. Attacks on the therapist at this point are not unusual; for instance, that her leadership is too strong or too weak—it's generally irrelevant which. An experienced group leader will view this behavior as a normal and healthy group phenomenon.

Why negative feelings first? Members may be testing the sense of trust and cohesiveness of the group, or discovering whether it's possible to disagree, or question assumptions. They might be afraid to voice deeply held positive feelings lest others reject these feelings. Some authorities suggest that group members may feel it is less dangerous to chance provoking a hostile confrontation than to experience emotional rejection.

If the group members feel accepted, and if a sense of trust and freedom is established, they begin, in *stage five*, to see the group as "their group"—for which they accept responsibility, and in which they can share personally meaningful feelings. Trust in other group members develops, and group cohesion is acknowledged.

The real group work happens in the *sixth stage* of development. Group members express honest feelings for each other in the present moment. They accept others and themselves, and then begin making real changes in their lives. Discussions are open and frank, and pretenses are dropped. Unproductive behavior diminishes. The group becomes a family, a corrective family in which normal relationships can be developed, as opposed to the dysfunctional family in which the group member probably spent her earlier years. At this point the group takes on a dynamic of its own.

None of these stages are traversed without courage, without daring, without risking. For group members who are fragile persons the challenge is real. *"Hanging in there"* is admirable.

The survivor's story that seems most relevant to me at this point follows. Sharon took steps so courageous that, later, she could scarcely believe that she had dared.

TERRITORIES AND TURF
by Sharon Gaines

I read *Speaking Out, Fighting Back* by Dr. Vera Gallagher in November, 1985. The book deals with adult survivors of childhood sexual abuse in their homes. It describes the tragedies of such a sad existence, and how such persons have overcome the devastating effects of abuse. It presents survivors' victories as they move out from a hopeless, helpless feeling to: "I made it!"

I plunged right into the book, reading it five times in three weeks. In fact, I could not put it down. I was amazed that women from all over the country were describing my own feelings. I was amazed to read the exact words said by my mother and stepfather, the same words as other victims' parents had said. I was amazed to learn that other women suffered the same frustrations as I, the same fears. But, above all, I was awed by the attitudes, behaviors, and responses to these women by the Good Shepherd Sisters.

I have gone to church all my life. I have heard all about God's love. Even when my stepdad was victimizing me, we went to church every Sunday. I did not understand God's love at all.

Dr. Gallagher wrote about a love that I want. That real love carried teenagers out of their pain. That love characterized the Sisters in these women's stories. Good Shepherd Sisters gave unconditional love to every person they came into contact with.

On December 12, 1985, I wrote a four-page letter to thank Dr. Gallagher for writing a book of hope. Oh, how I had needed a book like that! Then I decided to phone her.

The book jacket said she lived in Seattle. The operator had no number for Dr. Vera Gallagher. Did she have one for the Sisters of the Good Shepherd?

A Sister answered. "Could I speak to Dr. Vera Gallagher?" Lo and behold, she was on the phone.

"I'm Sharon from Indiana. I read your book. I want to mail you a letter. Can I have your address?"

I hung up, and couldn't believe I'd done it. Called a total stranger across the country. I never do things like that.

I wrote to tell Dr. Gallagher that parts of stories in her book are like my story. That I wish I could cry, but I can't cry. That I had turned off all my feelings long ago but that, with her book, my feelings were beginning to come back. That if she ever came within three hundred miles of Indianapolis to let me know because I'd come and see her.

But of course, she wouldn't let me know.

In January of 1986 Dr. Gallagher phoned me. She was invited to talk at a symposium on child sexual abuse in Cleveland. Would I come to Cleveland? I could stay with the Good Shepherd Sisters there. I couldn't believe my ears. "Do you want me to come? Really?"

February 20 was the day.

The closer the time came, the more afraid I got. I was afraid to meet Dr. Gallagher, afraid to meet the Good Shepherd Sisters. Afraid of being in their territory, on their turf.

I'm not a Catholic. I never met a nun. I don't know anything about them. What if I messed up? What if I did something stupid? What if I offended them?

On February 10 Dr. Gallagher phoned to double-check that I was coming. She gave the phone number of the convent, the address, and directions to get there. "Could I bring a friend? " I asked, too scared to explain that I was too scared to come alone. "I'll see you both in a week," she said.

Fear overpowered me.

I'd be in *their* territory, on *their* turf. Maybe I couldn't talk to nuns. Maybe I'd get in a miserable situation and not be able to get out. Maybe the Sisters would see me as I saw myself: dirty, ugly, unlovable, guilty, ashamed. I had hated myself all my life, and I figured they would hate me too. I didn't need another rejection.

But I *had* to meet Dr. Vera Gallagher. I *had* to find out if she is for real. I *had* to find out if the Good Shepherd Sisters are for real. And I had to find out for myself.

Susan and I departed for Cleveland Thursday afternoon. By the time we came to the freeway exit, I was a nervous wreck. We were directed to a house at the front of the Sisters' property. Trembling, I rang the doorbell.

And there stood Dr. Vera Gallagher. She hugged and welcomed us.

We talked for hours. I liked this Dr. Gallagher very much. My medication and nervousness made me very thirsty. "The fridge is full," said Dr. Gallagher. "Help yourself."

I was too wound up from meeting Dr. Gallagher to sleep. I watched T.V., exercised, and finally dropped off. Moments later, it seemed, Dr. Gallagher called us. We were going to the symposium.

I shadowed Dr. Gallagher. I felt safe with her. I watched her and did what she did. The day went well.

Back at the convent we headed for the dining hall. We served ourselves, and I looked for Dr. Gallagher. But she turned me around and said, "Let's meet some other Sisters." In a low voice I said, "I'm scared." She just smiled.

Sister Rose Henry and Sister Rose Catherine were very friendly; they asked about our husbands, children, work, and how we had come to know Dr. Gallagher. Then I decided to ask a few questions myself.

"Do you guys work?" Susan's mouth dropped open, and the Sisters laughed. "Oh, no," I said. "I know you work, but what do you do?" Susan laughed. "Keep it up, Sharon, you're doing fine."

Sister Rose Catherine, it turned out, is the school principal. And Sister Rose Henry is the Superior. To which I said, "Oh." I knew it was something important, but I was through with questions.

Almost all of Saturday we spent with Dr. Gallagher, sharing about ourselves. The group has given me a sense of self-worth, people who really care. It's my safe place. My territory where no one will hurt me. When I'm on my turf there, I feel safe. It's the home I never had as a child.

All our group members are adult survivors of childhood sexual abuse. We suffer the same hurts, hate, anger, confusion, and frustrations with our day-to-day existence. We don't have the answers but know we will be listened to.

Sunday morning Dr. Gallagher went to mass. Susan went to her own church. I waited, and after they left I walked over to the convent church to sit outside and listen. I loved the songs, felt at peace, and was glad to be alone outside the door.

I didn't want to go home. I didn't want to leave this experience. I didn't want any of this to stop.

Any of what? The feeling of acceptance with no strings attached. The sense of "You're important; I'll

listen to you." The implication of "You're God's child and a person of value."

It was for real.

Really for real.

My brief convent stay was the total reverse of my childhood treatment and the beliefs inculcated then.

I had learned the most important lesson of my life.

God had always known that I could not possibly comprehend a loving Heavenly Father. How could I? In his wisdom He had provided Dr. Vera Gallagher for me. In her and the Good Shepherd Sisters I have seen a reflection of God and His love.

I have seen God.

And God is love.

Questions for Me

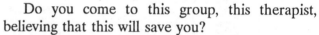

Do you come to this group, this therapist, believing that this will save you?

Have you tried other groups or processes that "didn't work?"

Do you realize that the only person who can change your life patterns is YOU?

Can you hang in there long enough to effect permanent personality changes?

Are you frightened by this new beginning? (So is everyone else.)

Can you make a commitment to the group process?

When you find group therapy painful, can you say so? Can you tell your group?

GROUP: A Family of Friends

- *There are benefits from sharing intimate memories and secrets with survivors who understand them.*
- *Relief from isolation and alienation is provided by a group.*
- *The group offers the gift of other women whom you can trust.*
- *Your feelings of guilt and shame spring from misinterpretations of your childhood molestation.*

Adults who were sexually abused as children, and who have not worked through the ensuing problems, tend to feel very lonesome and often are isolated. They are, in fact, hiding: hiding the secret, the guilt, and the shame. They feel, too, that they need to hide because, if not, they will be rejected—rejected because they are unlovable, stupid, clumsy, ugly, and on and on.

This extreme loneliness and isolation is dehumanizing, to say the least. Such persons lose the valuable contribution of human feedback, not to mention the social needs with which each person is endowed. We need to see ourselves mirrored in others' eyes; that is especially true for the adult sexually abused in childhood, whose early painful experiences have distorted her self-view. (I am reminded of D., a woman who told me she is ugly because of the black hair on her face. I could see no hair. "Who told you that?" I asked. "My father," she replied. "He always told me how ugly I was because of the hair on my face." I moved close and scrutinized her face. "You don't have any hair on your face," I said quietly. But she saw hair on her face, because her father had repeatedly

pointed out her ugliness because of the hair on her face. Such a woman needs friends who can assure her, again and again, that her face and complexion are fresh and lovely.)

For healing to occur, those women who were abused in childhood need to come out of their isolation and loneliness. To do that they need friends whom they can trust. Providing such friends is a primary function of the therapy groups I have formed for adult survivors of childhood emotional and sexual abuse.

Within these groups, survivors can share intimate feelings, stories, memories, and accounts of degrading incidents long buried in secrecy. They can talk at a gut level and feel assured that they are understood, not condemned. For most of their lives they felt so awful, so horrible, that they didn't dare reveal secrets. Unfortunately, the secrecy bored into their souls, making them feel that they, themselves, were the guilty initiators of childhood sexual abuse. They never stopped to realize that a five-year-old child cannot seduce an adult parent—mother or father, or other relative, or friend of the family. The only way such persons can discover that they are not guilty, not monsters, not perverts, is to tell their stories, expose their darknesses, show themselves as they truly are. When the group response is not horror but love and acceptance, survivors gradually learn that they are not bad. By degrees they learn, in fact, that they are good and lovable persons.

This process is not magic; it does not occur overnight. And it's subtle. Survivors whose self-opinions are changing often are not aware of the change—until one day with a shock they discover that they are really good people and have always been so. For the process to complete its course, it appears that most survivors need the kind of therapy group I propose (21-42 weeks). Sometimes group members may feel as though they are making no progress, but these particular changes occur gradually at the unconscious level—that level at which the pain buried itself.

Will such changes always occur? Yes, I'm sure of that. True love is healing and refreshing. Within the groups I watch true love and genuine bonding develop.

When survivors can recognize that they are truly good persons, and thus can accept themselves, they become free to see and hear and think what really is instead of the distorted versions developed in dysfunctional families. D., for instance, sees that her face has no hair and that she is a lovely woman.

After publication of my book, *Speaking Out: Fighting Back*, first-person stories of women who successfully triumphed over childhood sexual abuse, I got letters and phone calls from all over the country. At one point three women wanted to fly into Seattle to meet me; I asked them to come at the same time, and housed them in a vacation trailer we Sisters have on Puget Sound. One woman came from Indianapolis, one from New York, and one from a town in Alabama. They stayed for three days. After her departure one of the women described the experience for me. It provides an excellent commentary on the above words.

THREE DAYS IN SEATTLE
by Pearl, Ph.D.

The three days of sharing with Pat and Sharon were more helpful than a year of therapy. Through our mutual trusting and sharing I gained insight with the courage to take action, and developed more self-acceptance and self-esteem. As a member of ACOA for the past three years, I've appreciated the self-help dynamics and support. But I found that sharing with adult survivors of childhood sexual abuse filled a need not met in regular ACOA meetings. The difference lies in the degree of pain and the pervasiveness of hurt developed in children within dysfunctional, chemically dependent families, and the more severe, more problematic hurts and self-hatred engendered by incest and sexual abuse.

When Sharon, Pat and I started talking, we felt like old friends who knew each other when. I have numbers of high school and college friends whom I rarely see, but with whom I can reminisce as though our experiences were last week—but we have less in common than did Sharon, Pat, and I. We three compared the same experiences, similar

reactions, same kinds of current problems. True to national statistics, two of us were married and one divorced; all are heterosexual yet sexually inhibited; all gainfully employed and apparently successful in social relationships. Girls from normal families, loving sisters, might have similar feelings of comfort and understanding when they sit together over a cup of coffee.

I am socially very adept but terribly lonely. I belong to many clubs and count many friends—but sharing my true self, my deep feelings, the fears and experiences related to abuse, is terrifying. I'm never sure that I can risk saying that I was a victim of sexual and physical abuse. Often, sadly, I've been further hurt when somebody I trusted, some friend who liked me, somebody I thought I'd get support and love from, has responded with a patronizing air or has drawn back from me. "We've all had tough times in our lives," a Job's comforter may say. Or, "You don't seem to have been much affected . . .." "It probably wasn't as bad as you remember. . .." "I'm sure your parents didn't mean it . . .." "It happened so long ago; can't you just forget and get on with life?" What a blessed relief it was to talk with two other women who knew immediately and exactly what feelings I'm taking about when I describe an abusive episode. I'm still so vulnerable. Because I had to trust parents who were not trustworthy, it's difficult to judge the quality of persons now, to find out whom I might trust.

When first I dealt with the trauma of remembering the abuse, I often felt anxious. Sometimes, to release some of the horrible anxiety, I felt compelled to blurt out private information about myself to whatever person I was with. Most of the time, that was a mistake. Then I felt that my friendships were really a sham. If friends and colleagues knew the whole truth, I thought, they would judge me a defective, not important, perhaps disgusting person.

I was particularly hurt, also angered, by persons in the helping professions who thought they knew what it was like and then told me what I should and should not feel. (I have become more tolerant with the well-meaning innocents, and more particular with whom I share my time and memories.) Too often friends left me feeling more lonely, more depressed than before I confided in them.

Sharon and Pat understood how I felt. They too have told the "wrong" persons and then blamed themselves for a lack of judgment. My heart went out to them. I knew the pain of reaching out for a lifeline of help—only to have the person pull away. Sharon and Pat are the kind of supportive, loyal, and tolerant women who make the best friends. I felt pleased and relieved that they liked me. Maybe, I thought, I've got some of the same qualities that they show: compassion, pity for the powerless, kindness in adversity, real virtue.

I still need to share. I need to talk, talk, and talk about the abuse. I wish I didn't have to. I'm relieved that the compulsion seems to be lessening, but the fact remains: I still need to talk so that somebody says, "It wasn't right. Nobody should be treated like that. You didn't deserve it." Sharon and Pat understand the need for speaking out over and over. Because they experienced abuse they do not get dulled or jaded by the repetition. Someday, perhaps, I won't need outside confirmation and so much assurance. Someday I hope to be whole and healthy enough to know, to believe that I am good, that I did not deserve the abuse. I can see that Sharon and Pat didn't deserve to be neglected and beaten. What could a little child do that is so awful? Nothing. Little children deserve protection and love. If I can see that for Sharon and Pat, perhaps some day I can see that my own rights were violated. Perhaps I can believe that "they" were bad, not me.

With Pat and Sharon my sharing could be honest.

I didn't have to hold back my feelings or thoughts or choose my phrases so as not to shock or offend a "normal" woman. I didn't have to say a little bit of the truth, watch for the reaction, gauge whether my friend seemed upset or confused, and then decide whether I could open myself up more, share a little bit of my pain, my suffering. Or was it best to pull back into safe social conversation, commiserate on the petty annoyances of the day?

When Sharon and Pat and I got together I knew with certainty that their responses were not just from pleasant, kind people. Despite the difference in detail, they had endured, persevered through the same experiences. Ours was true compassion for one another.

To know that one is perfectly understood and accepted by another, is loved and appreciated just as one is, is a wonderful experience. It's probably what we all strive for, but seldom does another person totally accept us. With a thirty percent divorce rate, even marrying does not insure that lasting experience! We survivors and the shocking statistics of abuse and neglect in this, one of the richest countries in the world, is proof that most survivors never get the healing experience of meeting with our own kind.

Each of us has had professional therapy, but we are still coping with the handicaps caused by our abusing families. The struggle to build self-love by oneself is overwhelming. We need one another for a multitude of reasons. In fact, we three are very courageous women. We were unprotected babies who now need continuously to reparent ourselves.

The major problem that results from sexual victimization by a parent is the inability to trust or believe other people. Because, as babies, we believed that the parent was good, kind, and loved us, we denied evidence of the opposite: that the parent was not an adult but an overgrown bully-like child who got his or her way through the abuse of power, size, and fear. Children, especially if the abuse starts before they reach the age of reason, struggle to comprehend the reality. Even when we become adults we find that the emotional reality of childhood is elusive and fluid—if not comic and ironic. Let me illustrate.

Sharon described a couple of brutal childhood episodes. She wept as she finished her tale. Pat touched her shoulder; Sharon got up, went to the bathroom, and blew her nose. Still seated at the table I said to Pat with pity, "What an awful story. How could anybody treat a child like that, especially a beautiful, kind person like Sharon? Thank God, my story isn't that bad." Pat rolled her eyes and from the other room came peals of laughter. Sharon stuck her head out and laughingly said, "This is funny! While I was blowing my nose I said to myself, 'Well, my experiences were bad but, thank God, they weren't as bad as Pearl's.'"

We laughed, even as we realized that denial and minimizing are two kinds of defenses that continually crop up with us survivors. As Sharon says, evil is evil. How bad it is is immaterial; bad is bad. We need each other to remind ourselves that: it was bad; we didn't deserve it; and, we have every right to be angry and upset.

Most of the time our perpetrators, family, and friends—and ourselves—expect us to "forget about it, be Christian and forgive, grow up and stop living in the past." Only another survivor knows the horror of thought intrusions just when things are going well, for instance, in a loving moment. Only another survivor understands the panic when, at a movie or lecture, some remark, some scene, triggers a nightmarish memory. Only another survivor knows the terror of that sense of overwhelming powerlessness.

Besides the need for other survivors as I deal with the chronic problems of denial and minimizing, the togetherness with two more survivors helped me to identify, even accept, and deal with the emotional symptoms of victimization. The terrible guilt and sense of responsibility to the rest of the family, even to the perpetrator, seem ridiculous to the "normal" person. But only through listening to another victim's story, and then recognizing that I myself mirror those irrational emotional responses can I gain insight into the pathology.

Finally I learn that I'm being victimized again when I feel that I haven't visited my family enough, spent enough money on presents, cared enough about them to call more often. My husband said that if he had been treated as I was by my family he would cut off all contact. He doesn't understand that I can't. I am not strong enough. I'm too scared. Sharon and Pat understand my feelings, and they also encourage me to work toward more of a sense of my right to independence. Because of our meeting I finally took the step of writing to my sister and my mother, both of whom physically abused me severely, to say that for the present I would not visit or talk to them on the phone. But I still will write letters. For me, that is a huge step.

My guilts scream out, "What kind of sister/daughter am I that I can hold resentments? What kind of Christian am I?" Without the support of Sharon and Pat those guilts would drown me. When I pause to think, I know that I would not expect those two women to continue relationships with perpetrators; then I know that I need not do so myself.

We continue to hope, to hope eternally, that we will be loved by the only mother and father we've known. That kind of dream, in the face of brutal reality, is pathetic and pitiable. When I heard Pat say that her mother offered to take her back into the home after her divorce I could resonate with Pat's hope that, "Now my mother is giving me love, caring about my emotional neediness. She really does appreciate and love me." The hope was only a dream. Pat's mother opened her letters, read her mail, and gave her a pair of Pat's own used shoes for Christmas! Hearing that story, I can recognize the hopelessness of my painful desire for a mother's love; the despair of knowing, in my adult mind (but not in my childish cravings) that my mother is only continuing to manipulate me

into another setup for victimization, using me as an object to fill her own needs.

Since I wrote to my mother, terminating for the present both visits and phone calls, she mailed me an Easter card and a hand-crocheted collar. I do so long to look on these as peace offerings, thoughtful gifts for a loved one. Then I remember Pat's mother, and cry. And I cry again.

The struggle to own one's honest feelings, to accept and integrate anger, depression, bitterness, and resentment is difficult, even impossible on my own. Those of us who never learned as children that we have rights to protection and nurturing must struggle long and hard with the right to own emotions and feelings. It becomes somewhat less difficult to accept these burdens when I see my dear friends laboring under the same problems.

The time spent with Sharon and Pat revealed some of my good points so that I can continue to build self-esteem and self-love. I know I am a successful person but I do not always perceive it emotionally. My faith in the ultimate love of God has given me a strength of will that supports me in my struggle to become a successful survivor. I did not become a perpetrator, never dreamed of it. Instead I absorbed the pain and worked against all odds to create a happy marriage and healthy children. In Sharon and Pat I can see two fine strong characters. We three chose to live, and to live good, moral, redeeming lives. We have become spiritual persons who experience the redemptive quality of suffering. Each of us is a responsible, hard-working contributor to a society that did not even protect us. We are loyal to a fault. With ongoing help we can learn how to be loyal to our own humanity and to our own persons.

Those three days in Seattle were a gift from God.

Have you experienced a need to tell your story over and over?

Part Three

For Therapists

COGNITIVE BEHAVIORAL

GROUP THERAPY for Adult Women Molested as Children

The frequency and damaging effects of childhood sexual abuse have come into public consciousness within the past ten years. We have documented data about the psychological damage in adults of childhood sexual abuse, and the added damage of the traumatic, years-long repression of these incidents, but have developed few systematic and validated group therapy treatments for adult women survivors.

According to Martha Strauss in her 1988 book, *Abuse and Victimization across the Life Span*, the psychological consequences of sexual victimization have been a subject for debate in the psychiatric literature beginning with Freud's denial of childhood seduction and incest and his subsequent evolution of the Oedipal theory. Even now, women occasionally report that the therapist to whom they first went for treatment told them that no abuse had taken place; that it had been a childhood fantasy; and to forget it and get on with life.

The Long-term Effects of Sexual Victimization

Childhood sexual victimization has serious consequences later in life. In her research on adult victims of incest who were in psychotherapy, Judith Herman found significant levels of depression, impaired self-concept, and relationship disturbances in the women studied. Russell (1986) found that incest victims are at serious risk for being victimized again by sexual assault, including rape and attempted rape. Compared with nonvictimized women they also bear children earlier, are more likely to be separated or divorced, and are more likely to have no religious preference and to have walked away from their religious upbringing. Twice as many victims as nonvictims are unemployed. Russell reported a range of long-term effects: negative feelings and attitudes toward men, and the perpetrator specifically; negative feelings about their self-worth and their bodies, and increased fear, anxiety, depression, and mistrust of others. (Russell did not inquire whether the mothers of sexually abused children had themselves been sexually abused in childhood. In my personal experience this is often true.) According to Browne and Finklehor (1986), overwhelming evidence is accumulating showing that childhood sexual abuse is consistently associated with serious mental health problems in adult life.

Bagley and Ramsay (1985), Biere and Runtz (1987 and 1988), Gold (1986), Herman (1981), and Peters (1984) report that individuals who were abused as children are more likely than the nonabused to have symptoms of depression and anxiety, interpersonal problems and "acting out" behavior, suicidality, dissociative experiences, and sexual problems. Several writers suggest that these difficulties may be understood as a form of chronic post-traumatic stress disorder (Blake-White and Kline 1985; Lindberg and Distad 1985).

When Memories Return

Of the hundreds of women who have phoned, written, attended the workshops I'm invited to give world-wide, or been my clients in group therapy, all report serious psychological damage. Most of these women had repressed all memory of the abuse until their adult years. Typically these *survivors begin to recover memories between ages thirty-five and forty-five, while some begin to remember between ages thirty and thirty-five, a few before thirty, and a few after fifty.* Their presenting symptoms are usually a combination of some of the following: physical exhaustion, nightmares, flashbacks, eating disorders, alcoholism, drug addiction, dissociation, anger, rage, sexual problems, emotional and physical freezing, numb extremities, severe pain without organic basis, generalized fear, choice of a life-mate who physically abuses, sense of guilt and shame or unworthiness, grief, terror. Besides, adults abused in childhood may in turn abuse in some ways (other than sexually).

Adults molested as children (from now on referred to as AMACs) sometimes describe actual or feared attempted rape in adult life. Because the abused child develops a learned helplessness, she is vulnerable to further attack. AMACs may tend to put themselves in situations that risk rape, situations that most adults would avoid (Crewdson 1988). Most of the women who contact me have no religious affiliation. Some are underemployed or unable to work because of psychological problems.

A Shortage of Appropriate Therapy for AMAC'S

Of the hundreds who have talked to me, many AMACs find it difficult to locate adequate therapy. Many of those who phone report several years spent in therapy with little perceived improvement. Asked a Ph.D. candidate in psychology in Cleveland, Ohio in 1988, "Are therapists practicing on us?" The questioner is a survivor. She reports that she loses consciousness at times and is told that she then rolls on the floor. (Her description sounds like Kathy Evert's experience in her book, *When You're Ready*.)

Crewdson, in *By Silence Betrayed*, points out that psychoanalysts and psychiatrists who spend years studying schizophrenia and manic-depressive disorders are reluctant to do the "simple counseling" of patients sexually abused in childhood. Also, therapists may not ask about childhood sexual abuse in a client's background (Cole 1988). Or there may be an unconscious collusion between therapist and client to avoid mention of childhood molestation (if the therapist has this in his or her background and has not dealt with the problem). Finally, abusers in sheep's garments await the survivor; several clients have described sexual invitations from a therapist. One confided in a priest about her childhood molestation only to have him invite her out on a date.

Many AMACs get and describe excellent therapy. In Seattle alone I know therapists whose compassion and professional expertise are outstanding. Various kinds of therapy for AMACs are under development. In general, though, the provision of therapy for adult survivors can be improved. An AMAC who has sufficient drive—a quality that most AMACs lack because of an inadequate self-concept—can locate a therapist or counselor who will provide a healing therapeutic experience. However, most clients who join the therapy groups provided by Shepherd's Associates, Seattle, had previously sought treatment with little success.

Self-Help Groups. When many persons phoned from all over the country asking for help, I tried, but often did not succeed, to get them into therapy in their local area. In response, I started several self-help groups in several cities, contacting therapists in those areas willing to assist the groups. But usually self-help group members phoned me for an hour at a time—from the East Coast, Midwest, or South—with some regularity. I kept them on course but at the cost of hours of time. Therefore I tried to map out the progression of group therapy as envisioned, and offer workshops to therapists in Seattle; Auburn, Washington; Cleveland; Hyde Park, New York; and am engaged for workshops to therapists again in Seattle, Los Angeles, and Long Island, New York.

The Good Shepherd Program. For thirty years I was principal of Good Shepherd schools to which juvenile courts committed adolescents who had come into conflict with the law. In that position I worked with at least three thousand troubled teenagers. A high percentage had been abused as children.

My follow-up studies of 132 young women showed that eight or nine young women out of ten later made successful adjustments to life. I compared my data with those of other researchers of that period who followed up delinquents treated in foster homes, institutions, or by psychotherapy. The highest percentage of successful adjustment they showed for a comparable two- or five-year period was 5 out of 10; the lowest was 1.2 out of 10.

Reflecting on the treatment provided in Good Shepherd schools, I recalled that the primary emphases were on total acceptance, unconditional love, compassion, faith in the adolescent's potential, and education. We may have accepted our adolescents to a greater degree than professionals in general because of our religious orientation based on the biblical representation of Jesus, the Good Shepherd. The Good Shepherd leaves the ninety-nine sheep safe in the sheepfold to hunt for the one that was lost.

For victims who have not dealt with the issue of their childhood sexual abuse until later in adult life, I developed a cognitive behavioral therapy system based on the approach used in Good Shepherd schools. I hold the position that dysfunctional behavior is learned in dysfunctional homes or the dysfunctional atmosphere created by the adult molester if not a relative; what is learned can be unlearned; constructive and fulfilling behavior can then be taught and learned. This process is enabled and enhanced in group cognitive behavioral therapy.

Cognitive Behavioral Therapy: The Method

I differentiate between classical psychotherapy as most people know it and the cognitive behavioral system that I have developed for survivors. Classical therapy consists of a relationship between two people in which the therapist uses conscious and unconscious material to help the client change his or her life by alleviating the stress or problem. Cognitive behavioral therapy starts with the premise that the disturbed emotions evidenced by women sexually abused as children arise not only from the abuse but also from the destructive childhood conditioning and self-defeating education imparted by both molestation and the dysfunctional family atmosphere. In cognitive behavioral therapy the impact of destructive feelings and beliefs, such as "I'm bad, evil, guilty, dirty, and ashamed," is lessened.

Relationship to Traditional Therapy. Restructuring the cognitive system differs from traditional psychotherapy in several ways. It is relatively brief, often requiring only twenty-one to forty-two weeks of two-hour-per-week sessions. Cognitive behavioral therapy places more emphasis on producing change, usually much earlier. The cognitive behavioral therapist is much more active and directive than psychodynamic counterparts. Individual sessions typically are more structured and focused until reeducation is completed.

Cognitive behavioral therapy does focus on emotions, with the objective of getting clients in touch with their feelings, because that is how they learn what their irrational feelings are. We teach women how to change self-destructive, unconscious beliefs to a consciousness of personal worth and a sense of self-esteem and self-direction.

From that point we support clients in making their choices and determining their direction. The objective is to enable them to design positive, growth-producing paths for themselves. They become free—free from self-damaging choices, free from the incorrect messages of the past, free from the pain of feeling unloved.

Initial Contact. In a preliminary interview the client's ability to work within a group process is assessed. Some apparently very disturbed clients can function well in groups; some distract other members from the group process. The psychotic person needs more individual treatment than groups provide. Applicants take two tests: *Personal Orientation Inventory* and *Emotional Health Questionnaire*. Those survivors who are emotionally disturbed, suffering from one or, more likely, multiple areas of disturbance, but who can deal with life outside a residential treatment center, can be treated in structured group therapy sessions.

At the time of initial contact we do clarify that a course of treatment is not automatically ensured by the assessment. If we believe that Shepherd's Associates can't help this person, we make a referral, and try to explain the decision in a manner beneficial to the client.

Understanding the Dysfuctional Family. Survivors need help to understand how destructive systems in their lives interlocked to result in their victimization: the dysfunctional family, the childhood conditioning to guilt, the sexualization of their earliest formative years, the lack of predictable order that generated childhood anxiety—and the persistent denial of any of these. The child is traumatized but is likely to be told that the traumatic incident didn't happen; or if it did happen, the child made it happen; or yes, it happened, but that is what happens to children everywhere, always. If the child is told it didn't happen she learns to distrust her senses and feelings; if she is told she made it happen she has to figure out some way that she can control the incident so it doesn't happen again, but of course that doesn't work, so her level of anxiety mounts ever higher. She can't own anger or rage over the abusive incidents, because angry or disobedient children are not allowed in her home, so she learns to suppress and then repress her feelings. Survivors need to have the damage done to them in their childhood clarified through group discussion of personal stories, similar to theirs, told by real survivors. That material is presented in this book.

Children are bewildered in families where there is confusion over boundary issues, no locks on doors, where a father can walk in on an adolescent girl using the bathroom or taking a shower, or where a brother slips into a bedroom at night to abuse his sister. Children are even more confused in families with rigid, puritanical morals, where sex is not discussed but the child is sexually abused. In these latter families especially, family members are presented as extremely "good." The child internalizes this image and, as an adult, maintains a fixed and almost immoveable perception of the goodness of their parents. The resultant conclusion, of course, is that she herself is "bad." Such thinking changes the entire family environment and the child's situation; the child perceives a crazy world as sane. For example, one survivor said to me, "My mother isn't really bad; all she did was lock me up in cupboards for hours. And because I knew that might happen at any time, and I'd get a beating if I wet my pants, I learned to keep myself dehydrated."

Those survivors who deny both abuse and abusive parents cannot maintain the denial when confronted with the same or similar incidents told by another survivor. Examples are provided in this book. Others are likely to be related by group members.

Therapists need to be aware that occasionally parents do not abuse children emotionally and physically apart from the sexual abuse. In such cases it's possible that children may have a healthy love for their parents. I have not personally met any former victims who fit this description.

Since children need to have some kind of control in their lives, but have little or none in dysfunctional abusive families, they may find it more rational to convince themselves that they are "bad," and their "badness" is the reason for the abuse. The fiction goes something like this: "My bad behavior caused the abuse and it would stop if only I would be good." Since, of course, the abuse doesn't stop, the child becomes fixated in her personal image of self as bad. The result in the child-adult is guilt, shame, grief. Sometimes the child-adult engages in self-mutilation or marries an abusive spouse. She may be confusing love and abuse, or seeking to establish closeness with the abusive parent. Self-mutilation may be the result of abandonment or may be used to relieve anxiety. Such feelings are explored in this book.

Survivors are usually isolated, lonesome persons. Many overcompensate and outwardly appear to be successful, happy, and have many friends. Still, they feel desperately alone. Because they didn't learn as children that others can be trusted, and because they are usually incapable of developing intimacy, they can't share their personal concerns and feelings. In group they learn how to make friends, how to relax with other persons, even how to talk.

Survivors have great difficulty with boundary issues, often suffer from addictions, and usually have several symptoms of post-traumatic stress disorder. They generally blame themselves for whatever goes wrong in their lives. They describe themselves as "crazy" because they have panic attacks or flashbacks or nightmares. When they can examine those symptoms and understand their entangled causation, as is done in group therapy, they feel less distorted, less fragmented. But movement is slow. The process is not magic.

The Therapist's Role. Throughout the twenty-one-week period of the educational phase, the therapist asks, "How did last week go?" Depending on responses, a relevant topic from the many covered in this book is presented. The objective is to develop insight into the present problem as it originated in childhood, and to aid clients in their recovery of those childhood incidents or atmosphere that resulted in the current dysfunctional behaviors. Several more realistic responses that could be used are explored. That clients can change behaviors when they modify basic belief systems is emphasized. Most importantly, clients are enabled to experience and cope with their feelings of anger, rage, and vulnerability without becoming self-destructive. For this purpose the therapist is nondirective, encouraging free expression of feelings—provided that destructive anger is not directed at another group member.

The core of treatment is to enable the survivor to recall the abuse, describe it in a safe manner and place, and restore accurate meanings attached to the abuse. To this end she must first negate her denials and sense of guilt. As Alice Miller points out in her 1984 book, *Thou Shalt Not Be Aware*, the turning point for the client occurs when her rage is experienced not as meaningless, but as a response to cruelty. The work of therapy is to reclaim that traumatic past as a part of one's history and identity. With this kind of understanding the abused client can grieve and let go of both the trauma and the distortions in memory and affect that once were necessary for survival.

Not all clients feel "finished" after twenty-one weeks; the option of another twenty-one weeks is offered for those who choose it. Clients may need to express their rage and anger over, over, and over again until they have worked it through. They need to learn constructive ways of ventilating their angers. Again, material in this book will be useful. By the end of twenty-one weeks the group usually has taken on a dynamism of its own so that the therapist seldom needs to introduce new material. *The goal of the entire process is to enable group members to discover personal solutions to their current problems, with enough self-confidence to implement them.*

Assessment. At the initial assessment we give clients two tests to take, as mentioned above, requesting that they try to answer them quickly, without long thought over each question. We test again after twenty-one weeks of group therapy, and again one year after termination of treatment.

James Tracy, Ph.D., has done a preliminary study of the effectiveness of cognitive behavioral therapy with forty women who attended twenty-one weeks of sessions. He will complete the study after fifty women have attended the sessions. The study compares pretherapy and posttherapy scores on the *Personality Orientation Inventory*, a standardized psychometric instrument.

The preliminary results of the study show strikingly positive effects on the self-esteem of women participating in the twenty-one-week group therapy. This study is currently submitted for publication. Continuing research hopes to isolate specific elements within the therapy process that contribute to the positive changes. A complete description of the research may be obtained from Dr. Vera Gallagher at Shepherd's Associates, 11544 Phinney Avenue N., Seattle, Washington 98133.

Appendix

FOR GROUP PARTICIPATION

This book may be used in a variety of settings: by individual readers, by small discussion groups, by therapist-led groups. This section is designed to offer help and suggestions for group follow-up of the readings. It is coordinated to Chapters 1-12 and highlights those concepts and questions which are especially useful in group situations.

Chapter 1 **The Dysfunctional Family,**
wherein group members, with the help of other in the group, will begin to explore the origins of their own identities and self-evaluations.

Highlights

The purpose of this chapter is to help survivors begin to understand:

- a dysfunctional family;
- ways in which a dysfunctional family contributes to child sexual abuse;
- the inappropriate roles a dysfunctional family imposes on a child; and,

- the erroneous self-perception that a child acquires in a dysfunctional family.

Group Participation

In Chapter 1, readers are asked to complete this sentence: "I am innocent, but . . .." In the group therapy setting these responses should be read aloud to the other group members. Then, group members should be asked to respond to:

1. What did you hear about each member's opinion of herself?
2. Do you agree with the evaluation of herself? Why or why not?

Following this discussion, each individual member should be asked to respond to:

Now, what do you think about your self-assessment?

Some closing questions for group members:

1. What kinds of skills do you need to learn?
2. Do you expect to learn the needed skills in group?
3. Can you make a commitment of at least twenty-one weeks to group?

Finally, do you have questions about your group or your therapist? If so, feel free to ask every single one of them.

Chapter 2 Sexual Abuse: Who? What? Where? When?
wherein we explore together the frequency of childhood sexual abuse; why molesters do it, where, and when.

Highlights:

At the conclusion of this session you will have learned that:

- you were only one of many abused children;
- most sexual abuse occurs in the home;
- a child who looks for love and security does NOT ask for sex;

- memories of abuse are often repressed;
- sexual abuse of children cuts across all racial, religious, social, and economic lines; and,
- your life can still be good.

Chapter 3 A Survivor's Story,

wherein we explore together one woman's account of her childhood molestation. As you read and discuss this description, allow it to call your own abuse to mind. Every person's situation is different, but each is the betrayal of a child.

Highlights:

After you have read and discussed this letter, you will have understood:

- the power of the seducer;
- the helplessness of the child who is manipulated by the adult molester;
- the callousness of adults concerned only with their pleasure;
- that the molester usually has more than one victim;
- the child-adult's tendency to deny the pain; and,
- the endless efforts of the child-adult to win parental love.

Group Participation:

Here are some questions from the text to consider now in group:

1. Have you felt that you HAD to forgive your abuser? Has "forgiveness" become an issue for you? Have other persons who are important to you "blamed" you for not forgiving?
2. Each of us tends to deny and minimize feelings about abuse. Have you?
3. The letter describes physical, emotional, and sexual abuse. In which ways were you abused?
4. The "need" to love family is natural, even though the family abused. As a child and/or now, have you sought to love abusing relatives and, to do so, denied the abuse?

5. Each abused person needs to tell her story many times over. Have you told your whole story?

6. Are you currently in the process of "remembering"? If so, what incident have you recently uncovered?

Chapter 4 Boundaries,

wherein we learn together of the difficulties survivors experience with setting boundaries or limits. Because abusers invaded their privacy so early in life, survivors often don't know where one facet of life begins and another ends.

Highlights

After you have read and discussed this chapter, you will have learned:

- you, too, have rights;
- you deserve time and space of your own;
- you are responsible primarily for your own well-being and happiness; and,
- we can't really love others until we have first loved ourselves.

Group Participation

Here are some questions about your work, to consider in group:

1. Do you bring work home from the office?
2. Are you doing overtime without pay?
3. Is your work description constantly being enlarged upon?
4. Do others get promotions while you are passed over?
5. Have you asked for a raise?
6. Do co-workers hassle you?
7. Do you feel that you need to please everybody in your workplace?
8. Does everyone in your household share in the housework, cooking, child care?
9. How much free time do you have for yourself daily?

And now some questions about your self-care:

1. Do you take care of your health?
   In what ways?
2. Do you have pains for which you have not seen a physician?
3. If the physician said nothing is wrong, did you get a second opinion?
4. Do you get adequate rest?
5. How much daily exercise do you get?
6. Do you take time for yourself each day?
7. What are you doing to further your education?
8. Have throat and respiratory infections been a problem for you? Frequently?
9. Can you think of one nice thing you do for yourself each day? What is it?

Boundaries are important. Review this list of boundaries. Which ones were violated in your childhood? Do you own a sense of self, or "I am a person"? What roles did you take on in childhood?:

baby	dummy
scapegoat	juvenile delinquent
little mother	responsible one
little wife	failure
"brain"	parent to parents
slow learner	bully
daddy's girl	"always left out"
spoiled child	little miss sunshine
whiner	sicko
crazy	stupid
message girl	_____ if other, insert here
clown	

Chapter 5 Addictions,

wherein Gayle, a former drug addict, describes the force and fury of an addiction from which she won release only after years of struggle.

Highlights

After you have read and discussed this chapter you will understand:

- how and why addictions begin;
- why addictions have so much power;
- that addictions are used primarily to deaden pain;
- that the pain must be worked through in therapy (or other) before addictions can lose their power;
- that addictions, even the most stubborn of them, can be overcome.

Group Participation

Here are some questions from the text to review in group:

1. Are you addicted to alcohol, drugs, food?
2. How do you struggle with the addiction?
3. How may years have you had it?
4. Is your behavior compulsive in other ways?
5. How are you coping with addictions, if you have them?

Chapter 6 Stress and PTSD

wherein, Sharon Gaines, a survivor of childhood molestation, describes some symptoms of post-traumatic stress disorder.

Highlights

At the conclusion of this chapter you will have learned:

- about flashbacks;
- about the survivor's overwhelming sense of guilt and shame;
- that the body remembers;
- that fears can be overwhelming;
- that you can take control; and,
- that PTSD symptoms mean, strange though it may sound, that you are getting better.

Group Participation

Talk about the flashback phenomena in your group. Don't allow yourself to stuff feelings.

1. Review the stimuli mentioned in Chapter 6. Do any of these cause you to have flashbacks?
2. What kind of PTSD do you have? Discuss with the group your experiences with the PTSD symptoms noted in Chapter 6.
3. What actions are you planning to take to help you cope with PTSD? What will you do to get help if you need it?
4. What strategies can you use to reduce and control the stress in your present life?

Chapter 7 Lifetime Effects of Physical Abuse,

wherein we discuss the origins of that free-floating fear experienced by adult women who, as children, were the objects of severe physical, as well as sexual abuse. As you read, please allow into your consciousness the memories of physical abuse you may have suffered. As the reasons for nameless terrors are identified, hopefully they can be eliminated.

Highlights

After reading this chapter thoughtfully you will have learned that:

- the origins of free-floating fears are found in childhood;
- the reasons are real: you are not just a silly woman scared of everything;
- you need not be victimized by fear for a lifetime;
- resources are available for dealing with fears, and for discovering your own gifts;
- therapy for fears and phobias that result from childhood brutality can be time-limited and reasonably short; and,
- the only person who can really heal you is yourself—with a little help.

Chapter 8 **Why Guilt?**
> wherein we explore together one woman's account of the guilt that piled up, got stuffed down, and then exploded in a suicide attempt.

Highlights

After you have read and discussed this chapter you will have learned that:

- guilt makes many demands;
- anger turned against ourselves causes depression;
- persons who stuff guilt and anger do themselves harm;
- therapy groups provide relief for lonesomeness;
- the caring power of a therapy group leads a survivor out of depression;
- talking out the pain relieves anger; and,
- you, with a therapy group, have the power to resolve your own problems.

Group Participation

From the rules in Chapter 8, please select one or more that apply to you and your efforts to live the good life. Then write down exactly what ways these one or two rules are affecting you today. For instance, in what ways and times do you not permit yourself to get angry: at home, at work, with relatives, with friends, etc.? Discuss what you have written with your therapist or group.

Chapter 9 **Positive Emotional Growth,**
> wherein Sharon Gaines describes a part of her journey to health.

Highlights

At the conclusion of this chapter you will have learned that:

- progress at the beginning of your own journey may seem to move by fits and starts;
- you won't recover immediately;
- you are called on to be patient with yourself;

- for now, you need to forget forgiveness; and,
- peace and joy will eventually be yours to claim.

Group Participation

Explore in group whether you have been jumping in place, by responding to the following questions:

1. With what thought patterns?
2. Do you remember your childhood experiences?
   All?
3. Are one or more years of your childhood totally wiped out of your memory?
4. Do you feel guilty?
5. Does guilt result in unusual behaviors?
6. Why do you feel guilty?
7. Can you trust anyone?
8. Who? Who not? Why?
9. Would you wish to learn how to trust?
10. How to select persons you can trust?

Chapter 10 **Becoming a Person,**
wherein you come to realize that God created you and me as persons with a potential that we are called upon to develop. As a person you have many talents and abilities. You have a duty and a right to develop yourself and your gifts, and give yourself whatever time is necessary for that purpose.

Highlights

After you have read and discussed this chapter you will understand:

- the importance of YOU as a person;
- the need to give yourself time and space;
- the variety of ways in which you can be used;
- the importance of developing the talents with which you are gifted;
- the fact that you must respect yourself before you are respected;
- that love of self is the precondition for love of others.

Group Participation

Discuss in group the following questions from the text:

1. What good things do you do for yourself?
Every day:
Every week:
2. Do you ever take time to be alone?
When?
Where?
3. How many others do you take care of?
Grown children:
Parents:
Adult brothers and sisters:
Nieces and nephews:
Work supervisors:
4. Do you suffer pain but do not know why?
Where?
Have you seen a doctor about it?
If not, why not?
5. Do you feel that you do not deserve anything?
If so, who taught you that?

In fact, God made you good. You deserve good. Can you write how you feel about yourself?

Chapter 11 FUNERAL OF NOGOOD,
wherein we lay to eternal rest that figment of a sick imagination, the child, Nogood. We celebrate the sometimes slow, often invisible, progress to health made possible for you by group therapy.

Highlights

After you have read and discussed this chapter, and in the light of all the preceding chapters, you will realize that:

- you are a good person;
- the sick child you once believe you were never existed;
- the corpse of Neverwas should be buried;

- you can forget Nogood forever; and,
- you can devise a ritual to terminate the Phantom Child You Never Were. What will that be?

Group Participation

Here, from the text, are some points to reflect upon and, perhaps, to share with the group.

1. What persons constructed your false child-image? With what words, actions, glares?
2. Were you as a child physically abused? threatened? manipulated?
3. Did you come to believe that you really were that "bad" child?
4. Have you recognized the "Child-Who-Was-A-Lie?"
5. Are you ready for your false child to disappear?
6. What symbolic act could you plan in order to put that pretend-child away forever?
7. In what ways has group therapy helped you to distance yourself from that false child?
8. In what ways could the group have been more helpful?
9. In the future what good things do you wish to do for yourself?

Chapter 12 **Relationship with a Higher Power,**
wherein, DeeAnne describes her journey with God through painful abuse and healing.

Highlights

At the conclusion of this chapter you will have learned that:

- many persons on their personal journey to healing reach out to a spiritual Higher Power;
- most women sexually abused in childhood have walked away from organized religion because of the hypocrisy of their molester;
- some survivors have always known that God walked with them throughout the years of pain; and,
- some survivors begin recovery first with a relationship of trust in themselves, and then choose to seek a relationship to a Higher Power.

REFERENCES

Bagley, C., and Ramsay, R. Disrupted childhood and vulnerability to sexual assault: Long-term sequels with implications for counseling. Paper presented at the Conference on Counseling the Sexual Abuse Survivor, Winnipeg, Canada, February 14, 1985.

Blake-White, J., and Kline, C.M. "Treating the dissociative process in adult victims of childhood incest." *Social Casework: The Journal of Contemporary Social Work*. September (1984): 394-402.

Briere, J., and Runtz, M. "Post-sexual abuse trauma: Data and implications for clinical practice." *Journal of Interpersonal Violence*, 2: (1987), 367-379.

Browne, A., and Finkelhor, D. "Impact of child sexual abuse: A review of the literature." *Psychological Bulletin*. 99: (1986), 66-77.

Cole, C. "Routine comprehensive inquiry for abuse: A justifiable clinical assessment procedure." *Clinical Social Work Journal*. 16: (1988), 33-42.

Crewdson, J. *By Silence Betrayed*. Boston: Little, Brown, and Co., 1988.

Evert, K., and Kerk, I. *When You're Ready*. Walnut Creek, CA: Launch Press, 1987.

Gallagher, V., and Dodds, W. *Speaking Out: Fighting Back*. Seattle: Madrona Publishers, 1985.

Herman, J. *Father-Daughter Incest*. Cambridge, MA: Harvard University Press, 1981.

Lindberg, F.H., and Distad, L.J. "Post traumatic stress disorder in women who experienced childhood incest." *Child Abuse and Neglect*, 9 (1984): 329-334.

Miller, A. *Thou Shalt Not Be Aware*. New York: Farrar, Straus and Giroux, 1984.

Peters, S.D. The relationship between childhood sexual victimization and adult depression among Afro-American and white women. Unpublished doctoral dissertation, University of California, Los Angeles, 1984.

Rieker, P., and Carmen, E. "The victim-to-patient process: The disconfirmation and transformation of abuse." *American Journal of Orthopsychiatry*, 56:3 (1986), 360-370.

Straus, M.B. *Abuse and Victimization across the Life Span*. Baltimore, MD: Johns Hopkins University Press, 1988.

ABOUT THE AUTHOR

Dr. Vera Gallagher, a Good Shepherd Sister and a Certified Mental Health Counselor, has an M.A. in educational psychology and counseling from Seattle University and a Doctorate in Ministry from Graduate Theological Union, U.C., Berkeley. For thirty years Dr. Gallagher was principal of Good Shepherd schools for adolescent girls committed by Juvenile Courts. These adolescents had experienced a high incidence of abuse. Since 1984, Dr. Gallagher has worked with hundreds of women survivors in Seattle and across the United States who have phoned, written, or traveled to Seattle to ask for help because they had read her book *Speaking Out: Fighting Back* (Seattle, WA: Shepherd's Associates, 1985). Dr. Gallagher is frequently invited to give workshops around the United States and internationally for therapists, friends of survivors, retreat directors, spiritual directors, and women in general. Dr. Gallagher developed the structure of group cognitive behavioral therapy throughout thirty-five years of experience and thousands of contacts with adolescent and adult women molested in childhood. *Becoming Whole Again: Help For Women Survivors of Childhood Sexual Abuse* structures the healing process and thus will be of interest to therapists, survivors, friends, families, and the public.

RELATED MATERIALS . . . *from Human Services Institute*

A CLIENT ORIENTATION *to Group Psychotherapy*
Dr. Ivan R. Elder

This 39-minute video dramatization is an ideal material for preparing clients for group therapy. Clients learn how to relate productively and effectively to other group members. Nine basic rules for productive interaction are taught. Dr. Elder is on the staff of the Dorn Veteran's Hospital in Columbia, South Carolina, and has conducted supervised group therapy for over 12 years. This video is adapted from his book, *Conducting Group Therapy with Addicts* (HSI/TAB Books, 1990).
V1902   **$89.95**

ABUSED NO MORE: *Recovery for Women from Abusive or Co-Dependent Relationships*
Dr. Robert J. Ackerman and Susan E. Pickering

This book offers hope to women victimized by a confusing and seldom understood double jeopardy: involvement in a relationship marred by physical, sexual, or emotional abuse and compounded by alcohol abuse. Dr. Ackerman is internationally known for his work in alcoholism and the family. Susan Pickering is an expert of abused women.
ISBN 0-8306-3306-5   **$8.95**

BREAKING THROUGH: *Making Therapy Succeed for You*
Dee Gregory

If you are considering mental health treatment, *Breaking Through* can help you determine if therapy is the solution, identify the problems to be addresses, select the right therapist, and get the most from services of professionals. Dee Gregory is one of southern California's most widely consulted "consumer advisors" regarding therapists and therapy.
ISBN 0-8306-3549-1   **$10.95**

BROKEN BOYS / MENDING MEN: *Recovery from Childhood Sexual Abuse*
Dr. Stephen D. Grubman-Black

One in six males suffers from some form of childhood sexual abuse. This book reveals the consequence of male sexual abuse and the ways that victims can heal. It offers hope and encouragement to victims, and useful insights for parents, teachers, and mental health professionals. Dr.

Grubman-Black teaches gender role issues at the University of Rhode Island and conducts workshops for recovering victims of abuse.
ISBN 0-8306-3562-9 $12.95

DIVORCE IS NOT THE ANSWER: *A Change of Heart Will Save Your Marriage*
Dr. George S. Pransky

Dr. Pransky shows how the conflicts arising in most of today's marriages are illusions created by faulty perceptions and a lack of understanding of normal human emotions. The book identifies the most prevalent myths about what constitutes a healthy relationship and reveals how those myths actually increase marital discord. Dr. Pransky is a licensed marriage and family counselor who has worked with couples in private practice for 15 years.
ISBN 0-8306-3583-1 $8.95

MAN AGAINST WOMAN: *What Every Woman Should Know About Violent Men*
Dr. Edward W. Gondolf

Why is he so violent? Will he ever change? Do men's counseling programs really work? These questions are answered in this readable digest of the latest clinical findings. Dr. Gondolf is one of America's leading experts on violence.
ISBN 0-8306-9002-6 $7.95

STOP THE MERRY-GO-ROUND: *Stories of Women Who Broke the Cycle of Abusive Relationships.*
Milton S. Trachtenburg, ACSW, CAC

Poignant case histories reveal the true stories of five abused women. Trachtenburg, a psychotherapist for 25 yearss, works with women who are recovering addicts or adult children of dysfunctional parents.
ISBN 0-8306-8007-1 $10.95

TOO OLD TO CRY: *Abused Teens in Today's America*
Dr. Robert J. Ackerman and Dee Graham

Prevention and treatment of adolescent abuse is explained from the family perspective. The authors describe how adolescent abuse arises and focus on ways of recognizing and helping abused teens. Dr. Ackerman is internationally known for his work in alcoholism and the family. Dee Graham has been writing about women's issues for 17 years.
ISBN 0-8306-3407-X $9.95